# Mometrix
TEST PREPARATION

# Praxis® II

# Sociology (5952) Exam Secrets Study Guide

# Dear Future Exam Success Story

First of all, **THANK YOU** for purchasing Mometrix study materials!

Second, congratulations! You are one of the few determined test-takers who are committed to doing whatever it takes to excel on your exam. **You have come to the right place.** We developed these study materials with one goal in mind: to deliver you the information you need in a format that's concise and easy to use.

In addition to optimizing your guide for the content of the test, we've outlined our recommended steps for breaking down the preparation process into small, attainable goals so you can make sure you stay on track.

We've also analyzed the entire test-taking process, identifying the most common pitfalls and showing how you can overcome them and be ready for any curveball the test throws you.

Standardized testing is one of the biggest obstacles on your road to success, which only increases the importance of doing well in the high-pressure, high-stakes environment of test day. Your results on this test could have a significant impact on your future, and this guide provides the information and practical advice to help you achieve your full potential on test day.

**Your success is our success**

**We would love to hear from you!** If you would like to share the story of your exam success or if you have any questions or comments in regard to our products, please contact us at **800-673-8175** or **support@mometrix.com**.

Thanks again for your business and we wish you continued success!

Sincerely,
The Mometrix Test Preparation Team

**Need more help? Check out our flashcards at:**
**http://mometrixflashcards.com/PraxisII**


Written and edited by the Mometrix Exam Secrets Test Prep Team
Printed in the United States of America

# TABLE OF CONTENTS

# Introduction

**Thank you for purchasing this resource**! You have made the choice to prepare yourself for a test that could have a huge impact on your future, and this guide is designed to help you be fully ready for test day. Obviously, it's important to have a solid understanding of the test material, but you also need to be prepared for the unique environment and stressors of the test, so that you can perform to the best of your abilities.

For this purpose, the first section that appears in this guide is the **Secret Keys**. We've devoted countless hours to meticulously researching what works and what doesn't, and we've boiled down our findings to the five most impactful steps you can take to improve your performance on the test. We start at the beginning with study planning and move through the preparation process, all the way to the testing strategies that will help you get the most out of what you know when you're finally sitting in front of the test.

We recommend that you start preparing for your test as far in advance as possible. However, if you've bought this guide as a last-minute study resource and only have a few days before your test, we recommend that you skip over the first two Secret Keys since they address a long-term study plan.

If you struggle with **test anxiety**, we strongly encourage you to check out our recommendations for how you can overcome it. Test anxiety is a formidable foe, but it can be beaten, and we want to make sure you have the tools you need to defeat it.

# Secret Key #1 – Plan Big, Study Small

There's a lot riding on your performance. If you want to ace this test, you're going to need to keep your skills sharp and the material fresh in your mind. You need a plan that lets you review everything you need to know while still fitting in your schedule. We'll break this strategy down into three categories.

## Information Organization

Start with the information you already have: the official test outline. From this, you can make a complete list of all the concepts you need to cover before the test. Organize these concepts into groups that can be studied together, and create a list of any related vocabulary you need to learn so you can brush up on any difficult terms. You'll want to keep this vocabulary list handy once you actually start studying since you may need to add to it along the way.

## Time Management

Once you have your set of study concepts, decide how to spread them out over the time you have left before the test. Break your study plan into small, clear goals so you have a manageable task for each day and know exactly what you're doing. Then just focus on one small step at a time. When you manage your time this way, you don't need to spend hours at a time studying. Studying a small block of content for a short period each day helps you retain information better and avoid stressing over how much you have left to do. You can relax knowing that you have a plan to cover everything in time. In order for this strategy to be effective though, you have to start studying early and stick to your schedule. Avoid the exhaustion and futility that comes from last-minute cramming!

## Study Environment

The environment you study in has a big impact on your learning. Studying in a coffee shop, while probably more enjoyable, is not likely to be as fruitful as studying in a quiet room. It's important to keep distractions to a minimum. You're only planning to study for a short block of time, so make the most of it. Don't pause to check your phone or get up to find a snack. It's also important to **avoid multitasking**. Research has consistently shown that multitasking will make your studying dramatically less effective. Your study area should also be comfortable and well-lit so you don't have the distraction of straining your eyes or sitting on an uncomfortable chair.

The time of day you study is also important. You want to be rested and alert. Don't wait until just before bedtime. Study when you'll be most likely to comprehend and remember. Even better, if you know what time of day your test will be, set that time aside for study. That way your brain will be used to working on that subject at that specific time and you'll have a better chance of recalling information.

Finally, it can be helpful to team up with others who are studying for the same test. Your actual studying should be done in as isolated an environment as possible, but the work of organizing the information and setting up the study plan can be divided up. In between study sessions, you can discuss with your teammates the concepts that you're all studying and quiz each other on the details. Just be sure that your teammates are as serious about the test as you are. If you find that your study time is being replaced with social time, you might need to find a new team.

# Secret Key #2 – Make Your Studying Count

You're devoting a lot of time and effort to preparing for this test, so you want to be absolutely certain it will pay off. This means doing more than just reading the content and hoping you can remember it on test day. It's important to make every minute of study count. There are two main areas you can focus on to make your studying count.

## Retention

It doesn't matter how much time you study if you can't remember the material. You need to make sure you are retaining the concepts. To check your retention of the information you're learning, try recalling it at later times with minimal prompting. Try carrying around flashcards and glance at one or two from time to time or ask a friend who's also studying for the test to quiz you.

To enhance your retention, look for ways to put the information into practice so that you can apply it rather than simply recalling it. If you're using the information in practical ways, it will be much easier to remember. Similarly, it helps to solidify a concept in your mind if you're not only reading it to yourself but also explaining it to someone else. Ask a friend to let you teach them about a concept you're a little shaky on (or speak aloud to an imaginary audience if necessary). As you try to summarize, define, give examples, and answer your friend's questions, you'll understand the concepts better and they will stay with you longer. Finally, step back for a big picture view and ask yourself how each piece of information fits with the whole subject. When you link the different concepts together and see them working together as a whole, it's easier to remember the individual components.

Finally, practice showing your work on any multi-step problems, even if you're just studying. Writing out each step you take to solve a problem will help solidify the process in your mind, and you'll be more likely to remember it during the test.

## Modality

*Modality* simply refers to the means or method by which you study. Choosing a study modality that fits your own individual learning style is crucial. No two people learn best in exactly the same way, so it's important to know your strengths and use them to your advantage.

For example, if you learn best by visualization, focus on visualizing a concept in your mind and draw an image or a diagram. Try color-coding your notes, illustrating them, or creating symbols that will trigger your mind to recall a learned concept. If you learn best by hearing or discussing information, find a study partner who learns the same way or read aloud to yourself. Think about how to put the information in your own words. Imagine that you are giving a lecture on the topic and record yourself so you can listen to it later.

For any learning style, flashcards can be helpful. Organize the information so you can take advantage of spare moments to review. Underline key words or phrases. Use different colors for different categories. Mnemonic devices (such as creating a short list in which every item starts with the same letter) can also help with retention. Find what works best for you and use it to store the information in your mind most effectively and easily.

# Secret Key #3 – Practice the Right Way

Your success on test day depends not only on how many hours you put into preparing, but also on whether you prepared the right way. It's good to check along the way to see if your studying is paying off. One of the most effective ways to do this is by taking practice tests to evaluate your progress. Practice tests are useful because they show exactly where you need to improve. Every time you take a practice test, pay special attention to these three groups of questions:

- The questions you got wrong
- The questions you had to guess on, even if you guessed right
- The questions you found difficult or slow to work through

This will show you exactly what your weak areas are, and where you need to devote more study time. Ask yourself why each of these questions gave you trouble. Was it because you didn't understand the material? Was it because you didn't remember the vocabulary? Do you need more repetitions on this type of question to build speed and confidence? Dig into those questions and figure out how you can strengthen your weak areas as you go back to review the material.

Additionally, many practice tests have a section explaining the answer choices. It can be tempting to read the explanation and think that you now have a good understanding of the concept. However, an explanation likely only covers part of the question's broader context. Even if the explanation makes perfect sense, **go back and investigate** every concept related to the question until you're positive you have a thorough understanding.

As you go along, keep in mind that the practice test is just that: practice. Memorizing these questions and answers will not be very helpful on the actual test because it is unlikely to have any of the same exact questions. If you only know the right answers to the sample questions, you won't be prepared for the real thing. **Study the concepts** until you understand them fully, and then you'll be able to answer any question that shows up on the test.

It's important to wait on the practice tests until you're ready. If you take a test on your first day of study, you may be overwhelmed by the amount of material covered and how much you need to learn. Work up to it gradually.

On test day, you'll need to be prepared for answering questions, managing your time, and using the test-taking strategies you've learned. It's a lot to balance, like a mental marathon that will have a big impact on your future. Like training for a marathon, you'll need to start slowly and work your way up. When test day arrives, you'll be ready.

Start with the strategies you've read in the first two Secret Keys—plan your course and study in the way that works best for you. If you have time, consider using multiple study resources to get different approaches to the same concepts. It can be helpful to see difficult concepts from more than one angle. Then find a good source for practice tests. Many times, the test website will suggest potential study resources or provide sample tests.

# Practice Test Strategy

If you're able to find at least three practice tests, we recommend this strategy:

## Untimed and Open-Book Practice

Take the first test with no time constraints and with your notes and study guide handy. Take your time and focus on applying the strategies you've learned.

## Timed and Open-Book Practice

Take the second practice test open-book as well, but set a timer and practice pacing yourself to finish in time.

## Timed and Closed-Book Practice

Take any other practice tests as if it were test day. Set a timer and put away your study materials. Sit at a table or desk in a quiet room, imagine yourself at the testing center, and answer questions as quickly and accurately as possible.

Keep repeating timed and closed-book tests on a regular basis until you run out of practice tests or it's time for the actual test. Your mind will be ready for the schedule and stress of test day, and you'll be able to focus on recalling the material you've learned.

# Secret Key #4 – Pace Yourself

Once you're fully prepared for the material on the test, your biggest challenge on test day will be managing your time. Just knowing that the clock is ticking can make you panic even if you have plenty of time left. Work on pacing yourself so you can build confidence against the time constraints of the exam. Pacing is a difficult skill to master, especially in a high-pressure environment, so **practice is vital**.

Set time expectations for your pace based on how much time is available. For example, if a section has 60 questions and the time limit is 30 minutes, you know you have to average 30 seconds or less per question in order to answer them all. Although 30 seconds is the hard limit, set 25 seconds per question as your goal, so you reserve extra time to spend on harder questions. When you budget extra time for the harder questions, you no longer have any reason to stress when those questions take longer to answer.

Don't let this time expectation distract you from working through the test at a calm, steady pace, but keep it in mind so you don't spend too much time on any one question. Recognize that taking extra time on one question you don't understand may keep you from answering two that you do understand later in the test. If your time limit for a question is up and you're still not sure of the answer, mark it and move on, and come back to it later if the time and the test format allow. If the testing format doesn't allow you to return to earlier questions, just make an educated guess; then put it out of your mind and move on.

On the easier questions, be careful not to rush. It may seem wise to hurry through them so you have more time for the challenging ones, but it's not worth missing one if you know the concept and just didn't take the time to read the question fully. Work efficiently but make sure you understand the question and have looked at all of the answer choices, since more than one may seem right at first.

Even if you're paying attention to the time, you may find yourself a little behind at some point. You should speed up to get back on track, but do so wisely. Don't panic; just take a few seconds less on each question until you're caught up. Don't guess without thinking, but do look through the answer choices and eliminate any you know are wrong. If you can get down to two choices, it is often worthwhile to guess from those. Once you've chosen an answer, move on and don't dwell on any that you skipped or had to hurry through. If a question was taking too long, chances are it was one of the harder ones, so you weren't as likely to get it right anyway.

On the other hand, if you find yourself getting ahead of schedule, it may be beneficial to slow down a little. The more quickly you work, the more likely you are to make a careless mistake that will affect your score. You've budgeted time for each question, so don't be afraid to spend that time. Practice an efficient but careful pace to get the most out of the time you have.

# Secret Key #5 – Have a Plan for Guessing

When you're taking the test, you may find yourself stuck on a question. Some of the answer choices seem better than others, but you don't see the one answer choice that is obviously correct. What do you do?

The scenario described above is very common, yet most test takers have not effectively prepared for it. Developing and practicing a plan for guessing may be one of the single most effective uses of your time as you get ready for the exam.

In developing your plan for guessing, there are three questions to address:

- When should you start the guessing process?
- How should you narrow down the choices?
- Which answer should you choose?

## When to Start the Guessing Process

Unless your plan for guessing is to select C every time (which, despite its merits, is not what we recommend), you need to leave yourself enough time to apply your answer elimination strategies. Since you have a limited amount of time for each question, that means that if you're going to give yourself the best shot at guessing correctly, you have to decide quickly whether or not you will guess.

Of course, the best-case scenario is that you don't have to guess at all, so first, see if you can answer the question based on your knowledge of the subject and basic reasoning skills. Focus on the key words in the question and try to jog your memory of related topics. Give yourself a chance to bring the knowledge to mind, but once you realize that you don't have (or you can't access) the knowledge you need to answer the question, it's time to start the guessing process.

It's almost always better to start the guessing process too early than too late. It only takes a few seconds to remember something and answer the question from knowledge. Carefully eliminating wrong answer choices takes longer. Plus, going through the process of eliminating answer choices can actually help jog your memory.

**Summary**: Start the guessing process as soon as you decide that you can't answer the question based on your knowledge.

## How to Narrow Down the Choices

The next chapter in this book (**Test-Taking Strategies**) includes a wide range of strategies for how to approach questions and how to look for answer choices to eliminate. You will definitely want to read those carefully, practice them, and figure out which ones work best for you. Here though, we're going to address a mindset rather than a particular strategy.

Your odds of guessing an answer correctly depend on how many options you are choosing from.

| **Number of options left** | 5 | 4 | 3 | 2 | 1 |
|---|---|---|---|---|---|
| **Odds of guessing correctly** | 20% | 25% | 33% | 50% | 100% |

You can see from this chart just how valuable it is to be able to eliminate incorrect answers and make an educated guess, but there are two things that many test takers do that cause them to miss out on the benefits of guessing:

- Accidentally eliminating the correct answer
- Selecting an answer based on an impression

We'll look at the first one here, and the second one in the next section.

To avoid accidentally eliminating the correct answer, we recommend a thought exercise called **the $5 challenge**. In this challenge, you only eliminate an answer choice from contention if you are willing to bet $5 on it being wrong. Why $5? Five dollars is a small but not insignificant amount of money. It's an amount you could afford to lose but wouldn't want to throw away. And while losing $5 once might not hurt too much, doing it twenty times will set you back $100. In the same way, each small decision you make—eliminating a choice here, guessing on a question there—won't by itself impact your score very much, but when you put them all together, they can make a big difference. By holding each answer choice elimination decision to a higher standard, you can reduce the risk of accidentally eliminating the correct answer.

The $5 challenge can also be applied in a positive sense: If you are willing to bet $5 that an answer choice *is* correct, go ahead and mark it as correct.

**Summary**: Only eliminate an answer choice if you are willing to bet $5 that it is wrong.

# Which Answer to Choose

You're taking the test. You've run into a hard question and decided you'll have to guess. You've eliminated all the answer choices you're willing to bet $5 on. Now you have to pick an answer. Why do we even need to talk about this? Why can't you just pick whichever one you feel like when the time comes?

The answer to these questions is that if you don't come into the test with a plan, you'll rely on your impression to select an answer choice, and if you do that, you risk falling into a trap. The test writers know that everyone who takes their test will be guessing on some of the questions, so they intentionally write wrong answer choices to seem plausible. You still have to pick an answer though, and if the wrong answer choices are designed to look right, how can you ever be sure that you're not falling for their trap? The best solution we've found to this dilemma is to take the decision out of your hands entirely. Here is the process we recommend:

**Once you've eliminated any choices that you are confident (willing to bet $5) are wrong, select the first remaining choice as your answer.**

Whether you choose to select the first remaining choice, the second, or the last, the important thing is that you use some preselected standard. Using this approach guarantees that you will not be enticed into selecting an answer choice that looks right, because you are not basing your decision on how the answer choices look.

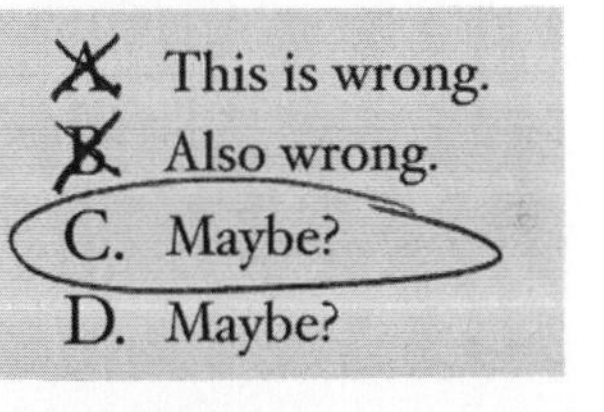


This is not meant to make you question your knowledge. Instead, it is to help you recognize the difference between your knowledge and your impressions. There's a huge difference between thinking an answer is right because of what you know, and thinking an answer is right because it looks or sounds like it should be right.

**Summary**: To ensure that your selection is appropriately random, make a predetermined selection from among all answer choices you have not eliminated.

# Test-Taking Strategies

This section contains a list of test-taking strategies that you may find helpful as you work through the test. By taking what you know and applying logical thought, you can maximize your chances of answering any question correctly!

It is very important to realize that every question is different and every person is different: no single strategy will work on every question, and no single strategy will work for every person. That's why we've included all of them here, so you can try them out and determine which ones work best for different types of questions and which ones work best for you.

## Question Strategies

### ☑ Read Carefully

Read the question and the answer choices carefully. Don't miss the question because you misread the terms. You have plenty of time to read each question thoroughly and make sure you understand what is being asked. Yet a happy medium must be attained, so don't waste too much time. You must read carefully and efficiently.

### ☑ Contextual Clues

Look for contextual clues. If the question includes a word you are not familiar with, look at the immediate context for some indication of what the word might mean. Contextual clues can often give you all the information you need to decipher the meaning of an unfamiliar word. Even if you can't determine the meaning, you may be able to narrow down the possibilities enough to make a solid guess at the answer to the question.

### ☑ Prefixes

If you're having trouble with a word in the question or answer choices, try dissecting it. Take advantage of every clue that the word might include. Prefixes can be a huge help. Usually, they allow you to determine a basic meaning. *Pre-* means before, *post-* means after, *pro-* is positive, *de-* is negative. From prefixes, you can get an idea of the general meaning of the word and try to put it into context.

### ☑ Hedge Words

Watch out for critical hedge words, such as *likely, may, can, often, almost, mostly, usually, generally, rarely,* and *sometimes.* Question writers insert these hedge phrases to cover every possibility. Often an answer choice will be wrong simply because it leaves no room for exception. Be on guard for answer choices that have definitive words such as *exactly* and *always.*

### ☑ Switchback Words

Stay alert for *switchbacks.* These are the words and phrases frequently used to alert you to shifts in thought. The most common switchback words are *but, although,* and *however.* Others include *nevertheless, on the other hand, even though, while, in spite of, despite,* and *regardless of.* Switchback words are important to catch because they can change the direction of the question or an answer choice.

### ☑ Face Value

When in doubt, use common sense. Accept the situation in the problem at face value. Don't read too much into it. These problems will not require you to make wild assumptions. If you have to go beyond creativity and warp time or space in order to have an answer choice fit the question, then you should move on and consider the other answer choices. These are normal problems rooted in reality. The applicable relationship or explanation may not be readily apparent, but it is there for you to figure out. Use your common sense to interpret anything that isn't clear.

## Answer Choice Strategies

### ☑ Answer Selection

The most thorough way to pick an answer choice is to identify and eliminate wrong answers until only one is left, then confirm it is the correct answer. Sometimes an answer choice may immediately seem right, but be careful. The test writers will usually put more than one reasonable answer choice on each question, so take a second to read all of them and make sure that the other choices are not equally obvious. As long as you have time left, it is better to read every answer choice than to pick the first one that looks right without checking the others.

### ☑ Answer Choice Families

An answer choice family consists of two (in rare cases, three) answer choices that are very similar in construction and cannot all be true at the same time. If you see two answer choices that are direct opposites or parallels, one of them is usually the correct answer. For instance, if one answer choice says that quantity *x* increases and another either says that quantity *x* decreases (opposite) or says that quantity *y* increases (parallel), then those answer choices would fall into the same family. An answer choice that doesn't match the construction of the answer choice family is more likely to be incorrect. Most questions will not have answer choice families, but when they do appear, you should be prepared to recognize them.

### ☑ Eliminate Answers

Eliminate answer choices as soon as you realize they are wrong, but make sure you consider all possibilities. If you are eliminating answer choices and realize that the last one you are left with is also wrong, don't panic. Start over and consider each choice again. There may be something you missed the first time that you will realize on the second pass.

### ☑ Avoid Fact Traps

Don't be distracted by an answer choice that is factually true but doesn't answer the question. You are looking for the choice that answers the question. Stay focused on what the question is asking for so you don't accidentally pick an answer that is true but incorrect. Always go back to the question and make sure the answer choice you've selected actually answers the question and is not merely a true statement.

### ☑ Extreme Statements

In general, you should avoid answers that put forth extreme actions as standard practice or proclaim controversial ideas as established fact. An answer choice that states the "process should be used in certain situations, if..." is much more likely to be correct than one that states the "process should be discontinued completely." The first is a calm rational statement and doesn't even make a definitive, uncompromising stance, using a hedge word *if* to provide wiggle room, whereas the second choice is far more extreme.

### ☑ Benchmark

As you read through the answer choices and you come across one that seems to answer the question well, mentally select that answer choice. This is not your final answer, but it's the one that will help you evaluate the other answer choices. The one that you selected is your benchmark or standard for judging each of the other answer choices. Every other answer choice must be compared to your benchmark. That choice is correct until proven otherwise by another answer choice beating it. If you find a better answer, then that one becomes your new benchmark. Once you've decided that no other choice answers the question as well as your benchmark, you have your final answer.

### ☑ Predict the Answer

Before you even start looking at the answer choices, it is often best to try to predict the answer. When you come up with the answer on your own, it is easier to avoid distractions and traps because you will know exactly what to look for. The right answer choice is unlikely to be word-for-word what you came up with, but it should be a close match. Even if you are confident that you have the right answer, you should still take the time to read each option before moving on.

## General Strategies

### ☑ Tough Questions

If you are stumped on a problem or it appears too hard or too difficult, don't waste time. Move on! Remember though, if you can quickly check for obviously incorrect answer choices, your chances of guessing correctly are greatly improved. Before you completely give up, at least try to knock out a couple of possible answers. Eliminate what you can and then guess at the remaining answer choices before moving on.

### ☑ Check Your Work

Since you will probably not know every term listed and the answer to every question, it is important that you get credit for the ones that you do know. Don't miss any questions through careless mistakes. If at all possible, try to take a second to look back over your answer selection and make sure you've selected the correct answer choice and haven't made a costly careless mistake (such as marking an answer choice that you didn't mean to mark). This quick double check should more than pay for itself in caught mistakes for the time it costs.

### ☑ Pace Yourself

It's easy to be overwhelmed when you're looking at a page full of questions; your mind is confused and full of random thoughts, and the clock is ticking down faster than you would like. Calm down and maintain the pace that you have set for yourself. Especially as you get down to the last few minutes of the test, don't let the small numbers on the clock make you panic. As long as you are on track by monitoring your pace, you are guaranteed to have time for each question.

### ☑ Don't Rush

It is very easy to make errors when you are in a hurry. Maintaining a fast pace in answering questions is pointless if it makes you miss questions that you would have gotten right otherwise. Test writers like to include distracting information and wrong answers that seem right. Taking a little extra time to avoid careless mistakes can make all the difference in your test score. Find a pace that allows you to be confident in the answers that you select.

### ⊘ KEEP MOVING

Panicking will not help you pass the test, so do your best to stay calm and keep moving. Taking deep breaths and going through the answer elimination steps you practiced can help to break through a stress barrier and keep your pace.

## Final Notes

The combination of a solid foundation of content knowledge and the confidence that comes from practicing your plan for applying that knowledge is the key to maximizing your performance on test day. As your foundation of content knowledge is built up and strengthened, you'll find that the strategies included in this chapter become more and more effective in helping you quickly sift through the distractions and traps of the test to isolate the correct answer.

Now that you're preparing to move forward into the test content chapters of this book, be sure to keep your goal in mind. As you read, think about how you will be able to apply this information on the test. If you've already seen sample questions for the test and you have an idea of the question format and style, try to come up with questions of your own that you can answer based on what you're reading. This will give you valuable practice applying your knowledge in the same ways you can expect to on test day.

**Good luck and good studying!**

# Sociological Perspective and Methods of Inquiry

## Sociology

*Sociology* is the study of how people relate to one another and how different types of societies are formed and maintained. Though its etymological meaning is "the study of comrades," sociology's use to mankind is often debated, and some thinkers (Marx, for instance) have questioned whether it can truly be an objective science. The use of the term *sociology* began only a couple of centuries ago with Comte, so it is still early in its development. Ideally, sociology gives society a mirror in which to critically appraise itself, and can recommend beneficial changes. Topics frequently considered by sociologists include community, bureaucracy, social stratification, family life, deviant behavior, and social change. Sociology is typically designated as a general social science because it does not limit itself to one aspect of human life, as do political science and economics.

## Groups, Dyads, Triads, and Aggregates

A *group* is any set of two or more people who maintain a relatively stable relationship with one another over a period of time. A group can be small, as in the case of a married couple, or quite large, as in a nation. A group consisting of only two people is called a *dyad*, and is considered the basic building block of society. A group consisting of three people is known as a *triad*. Groups are not to be confused with *aggregates*, which are sets of people who relate to one another only briefly and without effect: for instance, seven people all walking across the town square at the same time. The observed behavior of these people cannot be the subject of any meaningful sociological study since, unlike the members of a group, they are not connected by any social relations.

## Coalitions

*Coalitions* are formed when people unite to oppose a particular enemy. Typically, coalitions are formed when two or more weak parties wish to oppose a stronger party. Sociologists can often predict the formation of coalitions in cases where the success of several parties depends on defeating the ambitions of a dominant power. Coalitions are sometimes the only means by which these inferior parties can attain power (the imposition of their will on others). Although the formation of coalitions is studied intensely by microsociologists, coalitions also exist at the macro level, as in the case of nations uniting to defeat a common enemy in battle. Forming coalitions is one way humans have learned to prevent dominance by a single individual, group, or ideology.

## System, Interdependence, Equilibrium, and Functional Alternative

A *system* is a set of *interdependent* parts, meaning that a change to one part will affect every other part in the system. In sociology, a system can be as large as a group of societies, or as small as a group of symbols. Systems are important in sociology because they emphasize one of its core concepts: namely, that the whole is greater than the sum of its parts. This perspective distinguishes sociology from most of the other sciences. *Equilibrium*, when used by sociologists, refers to a congenial state of balance among the interdependent parts of a system. A *functional alternative* exists when a particular system has more than one structure to perform the same function.

## Social Networks and Cliques

A *social network* is the total pattern of relations among the members of a group. A social network is characterized by varying levels of transitivity: that is, consistent relations among all the group members. Intransitivity, disharmony in the social network, frequently leads to the formation of coalitions within the network, or possibly even the dissolution of the network itself. Mild intransitivity may contribute to the formation of *cliques*, small clusters of like-minded individuals within the larger network. Cliques can restore transitivity for individuals, in that they limit contact with potentially unfriendly parties. Social networks can become merely groups of cliques that never interact with one another, in which case the cliques become self-contained social networks in their own right.

### Nodes within a Social Network

*Nodes* are the connected units within a social network. In a given social network, the connections between nodes can vary depending on content, strength, reciprocity, and symmetry. The nature of the connection is considered its content; for instance, two individuals might be members of the same church and students at the same school, and so their connection is different than the connection of two people who are only classmates. The connections between nodes can also be more or less strong, and may display more or less reciprocity depending on how each node feels about the other. Symmetrical ties between nodes are those connections based on similarities, such as in age, class, or gender.

### Microsociology vs. Macrosociology

*Microsociology* describes any sociological study of the relationships among small groups of people, including one-on-one interactions. *Macrosociology*, on the other hand, is any sociological study that considers the behavior of large groups of people. These two ways of applying sociological methods are closely related, in that the behavior of small groups is influenced by broad cultural mores, and the behavior of the larger group is nothing more than the behavior of the small groups in aggregate. An example of the varying approaches taken by micro- and macrosociology can be drawn from war: a microsociological study would focus on the behavior of small platoons, whereas the macrosociological study would consider the behavior of entire armies.

### Cyclical Perspective in Sociology

Sociologists who take a *cyclical perspective* of their subject say that history repeats itself in cycles, and that humanity neither progresses nor accumulates more knowledge as it moves through these cycles. According to this view, societies have a birth, adolescence, maturity, decay, and death, at which point they are succeeded by some other society. During their period of growth, they have to be more creative and adaptive in order to survive. Once their survival is ensured, however, societies become conservative and stagnant, and eventually they decay. Many sociologists have disputed the claims of the cyclical perspective: some argue that it is an elegant theory not born out by the evidence, while others modify it to allow that individual societies may rise and fall depending on their innovation and attention to the lessons of history.

### Rational Choice Proposition

The *rational choice* (or self-interest) *proposition* is one of the fundamental assumptions of the social sciences. It asserts that people will tend to make decisions for their own good—specifically, to maximize their rewards and minimize their costs. According to both macro- and microsociology, humans will advance towards the things they like and avoid the things they dislike, even if this strategy is not clearly articulated in their minds. Many sociologists, however, argue that rational choice theory is limited because it fails to account for altruistic behavior, or behavior in situations in which an individual has no clear stake. Any sociological theory that depends on the rational choice proposition is considered to be a rational choice theory.

### STRUCTURAL FUNCTIONALISM

*Structural functionalism* is a sociological perspective that stresses the cooperative relationships between the various groups in a society. Sociologists who adopt this perspective tend to assume that all existing parts of a society are necessary to some degree, and that the society's progress depends on the quality of their continued cooperation. This perspective has been condemned by some as overly conservative, because it tends to endorse whatever system is in place simply because it is already in place, to the point that some structural functionalists have approved of crime as a necessary component of society. Most structural functionalists are less extreme, however, and see sociology merely as a method of analyzing existing societies rather than as a source of judgments or recommendations for future societies

### SYMBOLIC INTERACTION THEORY

*Symbolic interaction theory* is one of the most common ways of studying social interaction. Traditionally, sociologists adopting symbolic interaction theories place their emphasis on the symbols used by humans in communication. They study the ways in which human groups develop certain symbols to express feelings that are important to them, and the way status can be affected by the successful manipulation of these symbols. One of the core questions of interaction theory is whether individuals can have any freedom in a system of meaning that is external to them; that is, is it possible to express an individual truth in a language that must be agreed upon by the group? This question remains a subject of intense debate among interactionists.

### ORIGINS AND MAJOR PRECEPTS OF SOCIAL CONSTRUCTIONISM

*Social constructionism* is a sociological perspective introduced by Peter L. Berger and Thomas Luckmann in their 1966 book, *The Social Construction of Reality*. In this book, they attempted to demonstrate how individuals and groups construct their own reality, as manifested in social phenomena like institutions and rituals. This process of creation is ongoing, continually being reproduced and adjusted in social interactions. One example of a socially constructed institution is the church, which Berger especially has argued is a response to the needs of the psyche to have a higher purpose or order for its existence. Social constructionism is often thought of as a postmodern movement because it emphasizes the subjective element to all human life, and suggests that Comte's dream of a perfectly objective sociology is unattainable.

### ETHNOMETHODOLOGY

*Ethnomethodology*, literally "the study of the methods of people," is a sociological perspective that focuses on humanity's ways of understanding the world and expressing that knowledge. Rather than offer an analysis of society that competes with other sociological perspectives, ethnomethodology concerns itself with how humans make their own analyses. One way ethnomethodologists can illuminate these systems is by purposefully breaching normal conduct, for instance by placing a group of strangers in an unfamiliar situation and watching how they interpret it and work to maintain order. One of ethnomethodology's greatest insights has been the degree to which human language is *indexical*: that is, the degree to which words depend on their situational and grammatical context for their meaning. More generally, ethnomethodology has shown that human life is a moment-to-moment improvisation based almost entirely on context.

### CONFLICT THEORY

*Conflict theory* is a sociological perspective that emphasizes how the battles between systems of value determine the conditions of society. These battles can be large-scale conflicts enacted on the national scale (such as the conflict between conservatism and liberalism) or the conflict of individual desire with social norms. The conservative school of conflict theory asserts that society is held together by conflict, and that conflict is the natural release of the inevitable pressures in a social group. More radical conflict theorists, including Karl Marx, consider conflict the natural result of unfair societies. Sociologists of this branch of conflict theory point to mankind's history of oppression, enslavement, and exploitation, and suggest that only a massive social revolution can eliminate conflict.

## Sociobiology

*Sociobiologists* are those scientists who believe that human beings have endured on the planet because of the evolution of certain advantageous traits. Sociobiology has focused considerable attention on the nurturing behavior of parents; sociobiologists argue that it is due to an evolved tendency to preserve the continuation of the species. Sociobiologists have also studied altruistic behavior. They note that humans tend to behave most altruistically in relation to members of their own family. Sociobiologists speculate that this may be because of the desire to ensure reproduction by those with similar genes. Critics of sociobiology argue that it oversimplifies human behavior, reducing humans to genetically programmed robots.

## Phenomenology

*Phenomenology* is a wide-ranging philosophical approach that, in a sociological context, focuses on how people construct their own version of social reality depending on their means of understanding and experiencing their social world. This means consciously eschewing the large-scale social theorizing that characterizes the work of Marx and Durkheim, and focusing instead on the myriad tiny interactions that contribute to the construction of social reality. Phenomenologists are explicitly concerned with the things in the world as they are; they are drawn to areas of research like content analysis because of their determination to avoid giving human behavior any other meaning than that which it gives itself.

## Computational Sociology

*Computational sociology* has become popular in the past few decades. It uses computer technology to construct artificial societies, in which large-scale and complex social trends can be analyzed. Of course, this requires that the sociologists in charge of the programming have a keen grasp of their subject, and a willingness to consider only a few variables at a time. For instance, sociologists interested in game theory have used computer programs to try to discover the best strategies in complex games like chess and poker. They can then extract these strategies and test them in a non-controlled environment.

## Brief History of Sociology

Although the topics now associated with sociology had been discussed in political science and philosophy for centuries, they were first grouped under the heading of "sociology" in 1838 by Auguste Comte. The distinguishing feature of Comte's study of cultural, political, and economic life was its emphasis on society, rather than the state, as the prime unit. Spencer and Marx both made important contributions to the field, but the modern era of sociology began with Durkheim and Weber. Durkheim was one of the first to use statistics and research to explore social interaction, while Weber is better known as a theorist on religious topics. Sociology in the twentieth century has centered around three theoretical approaches: conflict theory, structural-functional theory, and symbolic interaction theory.

## Contributions to Sociology

### *Max Weber*

Max Weber (1864-1920) was a German sociologist and historian. He tried to create an objective methodology for studying the differences between societies. This effort, though flawed, was immensely influential on later social scientists. He also wrote extensively on societies as viewed through the lens of certain "ideal types," individuals who to Weber embodied the significant attributes of their society. His best-known work is *The Protestant Ethic and the Spirit of Capitalism*, in which he opposed Marx' theory of dialectical materialism (basically, the idea that progress is made though economic rather than philosophic conflict), and attributed the fantastic success of capitalism to the Calvinist emphasis on work ethic and frugality.

*Antipositivism* and *verstehen* are two concepts introduced by Max Weber. Weber argued that the method of sociology had to be *antipositive*; that is, it had to be comprised of different elements than those used in the natural sciences. This was a rejection of Comte, who had claimed that sociology could follow the same methodology used in fields like chemistry and biology. *Verstehen*, which means "understanding" in German, is the process whereby outside observers use their own standards to consider another group of people. Many sociologists claim that this is the only way for knowledge to be gathered, but critics counter that it is impossible for one culture ever to understand another fully. Weber has even been accused of cultural arrogance for assuming that his culture's set of analytical tools is suitable to judge every other culture.

### *Karl Marx*

Karl Marx (1818-1883) was a German economic theorist who, along with his collaborator Freidrich Engels, developed the major principles of modern socialism. Marx wrote much of his work in emulation of and as a rebuttal to Hegel, as evidenced most clearly by his theory of dialectical materialism (the ongoing progress of society through economic competition). According to Marx, economic interest is the driving force behind human history, and determines all the social, material, intellectual, and spiritual aspects of human life. He outlined the case for destroying this capitalist model in favor of a classless, socialist society in the *Communist Manifesto*. A more complete account of his ideas, however, can be found in *Das Kapital*. These ideas were essential to the philosophy of Lenin, and hence in the formation of Russian communism.

### *Emile Durkheim*

Emile Durkheim (1857-1951) was a French thinker who made some important contributions to sociology, most notably on the subjects of suicide, the division of labor, and religion. Perhaps because he grew up during a tumultuous time in France, he spent much of his career making the case for strong authority in society. Controversially, he claimed that the concept of God was a misplaced societal urge for order and stable authority, and that organized religions were clever solutions to the problems of managing a society rather than expressions of divine truth. He contrasted this kind of mechanical solidarity with what he called organic solidarity, which he said would emerge if the labor force were divided in such a way that the members of society were dependent on one another.

### *Vilfredo Pareto*

Vilfredo Pareto (1848-1923) was an Italian economist and sociologist whose ideas are often considered to be seminal in the creation of fascism. He used the methods of economics to analyze individual choice and the distribution of income. One of his most famous notions is of the society that can be improved for one person without inconveniencing anyone else; such an improvement is known as *Pareto efficiency*. Pareto also developed the *indifference curve*, to describe situations in which consumers do not prefer one product to another. He is perhaps most famous for observing that in most societies a large proportion of property is owned by a small proportion of the population, an observation that has come to be known as the *Pareto principle.*

### George Herbert Mead

George Herbert Mead (1863-1931) was the American philosopher and sociologist who is considered to be the founder of *symbolic interactionism.* Mead, along with Weber, viewed sociology through the lens of antipositivism, and focused on the way that individual identity is formed through social experiences. Specifically, Mead believed that humans could only be understood in terms of the systems of thought, or *symbols*, that they use to communicate with each other. To Mead, there was no such thing as scientific objectivity in sociology, because the human mind cannot imagine a system of observation that does not contain the subjective element. Mead spent much of his career studying the ways in which symbolic languages are developed and maintained in society.

### Herbert Spencer

Herbert Spencer (1820-1903) was an English philosopher whose *Principles of Sociology* helped establish the discipline as a legitimate subject for study. In this massive three-volume work, Spencer charted the individual's development and increasing freedom from the constrictions of society. He suggested also that conventional morality is less a God-given template for behavior than a necessary means of survival in a competitive society. According to Spencer, humans were evolving to become more interdependent not out of any natural affinity, but out of a refinement of the survival instinct. These ideas lead many to consider Spencer the originator of *social Darwinism,* although some of his views oppose what is often meant by that expression.

### Auguste Comte

Auguste Comte (1798-1857) was the French philosopher and social reformer credited with introducing sociology as a legitimate science. He asserted that sociology was the most complex and least easily applicable science, but that it was the one most worthy of study. He is responsible also for delineating the Three Phases (Theological, Metaphysical, and Scientific or Positive) through which every science develops. Comte hoped to make sociology a positive science: that is, one in which phenomena are described on the basis of observation and experimentation rather than myth. With the idealism characteristic of the Enlightenment, he believed this would enable nations and individuals to find harmony with one another.

## Careers in Sociology

For the most part, individuals trained in sociology work as teachers, researchers, or clinical sociologists. Sociological research is conducted in a number of different institutions: academia, government agencies, and interest groups, to name a few. Many individuals are in private sociological practice, meaning that they conduct research and evaluations of social groups on a contractual basis. Clinical sociologists work with a broad spectrum of groups, from small offices to nations. Their role may be as a counselor, consultant, advisor, or analyst. The main goal of clinical sociology, whatever its setting, is to discover the source of problems between people and to help reach a solution.

## Quantitative and Qualitative Research

Sociological research can generally be divided into two types: quantitative and qualitative. In *quantitative research*, sociologists measure the instances of a particular phenomenon and use statistical measures to assess its place within the society. Durkheim's work on suicide, for instance, could be considered quantitative research; even though he lacked the modern aid of the computer, Durkheim relied on statistics and large-scale measurements to make his points. *Qualitative research* is typically more concerned with examining a particular social phenomenon in great detail.

It is interested in discovering the meaning of the phenomenon by finding out how people conceive of it, how they describe it, and how it is done. Qualitative research eschews statistical measures, instead focusing on interviews, observation, and participation.

## Ethnographies and Panel Studies

*Ethnography* is a form of observational research in which sociologists collect data by studying people in their natural environment. Typically, ethnographies are created over a long period. The goal of ethnography is to observe human interaction as it actually happens, rather than to manufacture interactions in a laboratory. The sociologist then tries to describe or interpret the observed behavior. A *panel study* is a public opinion survey in which the same respondents are interviewed several times. Sociologists use panel studies to discover how people understand their social world, and how this understanding changes over time. Typically, panel studies are used to explore the values and norms that endure in a society, rather than the issues of the day.

## Comparative Research and Cross-Cultural Research

Many sociological studies are comparisons between different groups or societies. *Comparative research* may incorporate any of the various tools of research. When sociologists conduct studies of societies other than the one that they themselves live in, it is called *cross-cultural research*. There is continual debate in sociology over whether it is possible to understand a foreign culture on its own terms or, on the other hand, to apply fairly the standards of one society to another. Sociologists consciously guard against the tendency to describe other cultures in the categories and terms to which the sociologists are accustomed. Nevertheless, cross-cultural research is becoming increasingly common in sociology, as globalization brings diverse societies into closer contact with one another.

## Types of Observation

*Non-participant observation* is a research technique in which sociologists study behavior very closely, but do not actually engage in the behavior they are studying. Although the subjects are aware that they are being studied, they are not encouraged to act any particular way. A *covert participant observation* is a way of gathering sociological data by observing human behavior without the subjects knowing that they are being observed, and without the sociologists identifying themselves as such. In *overt participation observation*, sociologists study behavior by joining in on it. Oftentimes, this requires that the sociologist actually spend years cultivating the trust of the group and earning a role within it. In this kind of research, the subjects are aware that they are being observed.

## Nonexperimental Research and Field Observation Research

Most sociological research is *nonexperimental research*, meaning it is not conducted in controlled laboratory settings. *Field observation research* is any study of people in their normal, everyday environments, rather than in a laboratory. When conducting field research, sociologists do not always make themselves known to the subjects of their observation. Sometimes, sociologists select the variables to be studied after the observations are made (known as *ex post facto research*); and other times, they conduct studies in which the independent variable is not directly manipulated (known as *quasi-experimental research*). Both the *ex post facto* and quasi-experimental research methods are characterized as *passive research*, because they require the observer to adjust according to the results, rather than vice versa.

## Survey Research

*Survey research* (also known as public opinion polling) is a common form of sociological research in which a sample population is questioned directly. This questioning is often done in person, though it can also be accomplished over the phone, by mail, or over the Internet. Survey research is especially effective in measuring opinions on subjects unlikely to come before a vote. For instance, the American public does not vote on whether or not to go to war, but opinion on this subject is of great interest to politicians and sociologists alike. The relative accuracy and effectiveness of a survey depends on posing the right questions to the right people.

### SURVEY POPULATIONS, SAMPLES, AND RANDOM SAMPLES

The *population* of a survey is the total group of people who have whatever characteristic the sociologist is studying. In a survey of opinions on abortion, for instance, the sociologist may get different results depending on whether his population is all people, all women, or all women who have had abortions. Of course, few populations are small enough for every member to be interviewed in person, so sociologists use what is known as a *sample*. In a survey, a sample is a limited group within the total population being studied. Sociologists strive to select a sample that fairly represents the larger society. A *random sample* is one in which every person within the population has an equal chance of being selected for the survey.

### CONSTRUCTION OF SURVEY QUESTIONS

Sociologists spend a great deal of time trying to construct survey questions that will produce reliable and accurate results. Wording is very important; studies have shown, for instance, that questions asking whether something should be "forbidden" elicit different responses than those that ask whether the same thing should be "allowed." The sequence of the questions asked is also important, as the issues raised by previous questions may affect subsequent responses. Also, sociologists must decide whether their questions should receive a *closed response*, in which the respondent chooses his or her answer from a list, or an *open response*, in which the answer is given in the respondent's own words.

### INTERVIEW IN A SOCIOLOGICAL CONTEXT

An *interview* is a conversation in which a researcher and another person discuss a topic. An interview format is typically informal, so that the researcher may adjust the questions or the tone to suit the mood and character of the respondent. Interviews may have more or less structure. In an unstructured interview, no topics or questions are predetermined, and so the conversation wanders where it will. In a semi-structured interview, the researcher has a general idea of what topics he or she would like to cover, but maintains a great deal of flexibility throughout the process. In a structured interview, the precise wording and order of the questions is decided well in advance. The somewhat improvisatory nature of most interviews means that they often say as much about the researcher as about the respondent.

### CONTENT ANALYSIS AND CODING FRAMES

*Content analysis* is a research method employed by sociologists, in which interpersonal communication is organized and studied to determine both its explicit and implicit meaning. The sociologist Harold Lasswell said the purpose of content analysis was to ask, "Who says what, to whom, why, to what extent, and with what effect?" Many sociologists tout the low invasiveness of content analysis as a sign that it is able to attain pure information. One of the problems with it, however, is that it tends to generate huge amounts of information: a simple study of the verbal communication in a household, for instance, can quickly become unmanageable. For this reason, sociologists have developed some helpful *coding frames*, or means of categorizing information (for example, by keyword) as it is collected. Of course, the particular coding frames used affect the quality of the study.

## HISTORICAL RESEARCH AND SECONDARY ANALYSIS

Sociologists often draw upon historical records during research. *Historical research* is frequently used to compare some contemporary social phenomenon with instances of that phenomenon from the past. In the case of social revolutions, for example, sociologists must refer to historical sources frequently, since revolutions only happen every once in a while. For sociology, the danger of ignoring the historical record is that it may lead to false generalizations based on a small sample size. In performing historical research, sociologists frequently revisit documents that were created for some other purpose, like church records, old newspapers, diaries, or government statistics. The use of these sources in sociological research is known as *secondary analysis*.

## QUALIFICATIONS OF SOCIOLOGY AS SOCIAL SCIENCE

Sociology is considered one of the social sciences because it adheres to the *scientific method*: the traditional steps for acquiring knowledge in a field of scientific inquiry. The first step in the scientific method is observation, followed by the posing of a specific question. After this, the scientist offers a *hypothesis*, or educated guess as to the answer, and proceeds to test that hypothesis through experiment. In sociology, an experiment may take the form of artificially engineered social situations or close observation of natural group behavior. If a hypothesis is proven to be correct, even when the scientist actively seeks contradictory evidence, it may become a scientific *theory*. There has always been a great deal of debate about whether sociological research can be considered scientific research, so sociologists are very careful to honor the precepts of the scientific method.

## EXPERIMENTS

In sociology, an *experiment* is a controlled form of research in which a sociologist creates conditions that are ideal for study. This is done by maintaining control over all the aspects of a situation and then carefully altering one factor, known as the *independent variable*. As the researcher alters the independent variable, he or she notes the effects of this change on the *dependent variable*. *Experimental controls* are the steps taken by the scientist to ensure that no outside factors intrude upon the purity of the experiment. A scientist performs a *replication* of an earlier experiment when he or she wants to demonstrate that the results of the prior experiment can be duplicated at a different time or place.

## DATA, MEAN, MEDIAN, AND MODE

In sociology, *data* are defined as any facts, statistics, research, or other pieces of observation that are organized and used to develop sociological theories. Sociologists often describe the numerical data they have collected by giving the mean, median, or mode. The *mean* is the average of a list of data. It is calculated by adding all the figures together, and then dividing by the total number of figures. The *median* is the number that falls in the middle of a sequence of figures; in the series 1, 3, 6, 8, 9, for instance, the median number is 6. The *mode* of a series of data is the figure that occurs most often.

## STANDARD DEVIATION AS IT RELATES TO RESEARCH

In order to test a hypothesis, a sociologist needs to conduct research and acquire data. Data can be any facts, statistics, or study results that are relevant to the experiment. Data does not arrive with directions for how to interpret it, however; once it is collected, the sociologist must decide how to accurately and effectively use it. The *standard deviation* is the statistical measure of distance between other recorded data and the mean, or average. For example, if a sociologist has collected information on the number of divorces in a society, he will want to compare his data with previous findings to make sure that his data is believable. Data that falls outside the standard deviation frequently indicates an error in the collection process.

## Indicator and Operational Definition

An *indicator* is anything that is easily measured and seems to be proportionate to some more complex (and hence more difficult to measure) variable. For example, sociologists who are attempting to measure the social integration of a society might use indicators like the divorce rate, crime rate, membership in community groups, or population density. If one of these variables were determined to be an accurate indicator of social integration, it could become an operational definition. An *operational definition* is a measurable indicator for one of the variables included in a hypothesis. After a sociologist has determined a good operational definition, he or he is ready to select the most effective research method for measuring this indicator.

## Correlation, Correlation Coefficient and Spurious Correlation

When sociologists notice a repeated connection between two variables over time, they refer to it as a *correlation*. There is a correlation, for example, between rainy weather and the number of people carrying umbrellas. A *correlation coefficient* is a number between zero and one that describes the strength of a certain correlation. A *spurious correlation* is one that seems to show a correlation between two variables, when in fact there is no causal connection between the two. If, for instance, it happened that the number of people wearing orange went up at the same time the stock market plummeted, it would most likely be spurious to claim that one had an effect on the other.

## Randomization and Tests of Significance

Randomization and tests of significance are two of the tools that sociologists use to ensure that observed correlations are trustworthy. *Randomization* is the random selection of participants in an experiment, with the interest of maintaining experimental groups with normal characteristics. By making selection random, sociologists intend to prevent any group from having wildly different members, and thus potentially skewing that group's reaction to the independent variable. A *test of significance* is a computation of the odds that a correlation occurred by chance; sociologists typically require that the odds of a chance finding be less than 5% before they will trust a correlation.

## Validity and Reliability in Research

Like any scientific experiment, sociological studies must be judged by the community for their validity and reliability. The *validity* of a study is the degree to which the study manages to describe what it is attempting to describe. A classic example of an invalid study is one that uses a faulty operational definition: a study that tries to gauge social integration by measuring life expectancy, perhaps. The *reliability* of a study is the degree to which it can be closely replicated by other researchers. Studies that do not yield the same results time after time are useless in the construction of scientific theories, and usually suggest some kind of error in the construction of the experiment.

## Theory and Method

The final step in the scientific method used by sociology is the creation of theories. A *theory* is a logical attempt to take the information gathered by an experiment and describe how it fits into the larger picture developed by previous experimentation. The degree to which a theory asserts a causal relationship varies: some theories make bold statements regarding the relationships between social phenomena, while others simply place their findings within the context of existing knowledge on the subject. In any case, a theory should point out some areas for future research.

This research will in turn give rise to new theories, or to modifications of the old theory, which will then lead to new research, until sociologists feel the topic has been exhausted.

## Possible Dangers of Sociological Research

Though most sociologists guard against harming their subjects, there is the potential for damage when research is performed. Any experiments that involve deceiving or manipulating subjects have the potential to cause psychological damage. Those studies that concern private aspects of an individual's life must also be handled with care by investigating sociologists. Studies that focus on underprivileged or less intelligent individuals are sometimes dangerous for sociologists, who run the risk of confusing and coercing their subjects, perhaps unintentionally. Lastly, studies in which the results will be published or otherwise made known to the society at large can be dangerous to the participants, who may feel their privacy has been violated.

## Solutions to the Ethical Problems of Sociological Research

Sociologists take a number of steps to ensure that their research is not injurious to the individual participants or to the society at large. First of all, most sociological studies are conducted with full disclosure; that is, the participants know that they are part of a study. Moreover, studies almost always use voluntary participants. Sociologists often grant anonymity to subjects who prefer it, and they may also provide confidentiality forms so that subjects know important information will not be passed around to their disadvantage. In academic research, certain controversial topics (like illegal or immoral activities) may only be researched with the approval of an ethics committee. A similar committee operates in most university sociology departments to critique the methodology of all the research that is conducted there.

## Altruism and Egoism

One exception to the rational choice proposition (which states that individuals will always act in what they believe to be their own interest) is the case of *altruism*, behavior motivated by rewards for others. Altruistic behavior can sometimes even be injurious to oneself. Comte introduced altruism as the opposite of *egoism*, which is essentially rational choice theory made into a personal philosophy. An egoist believes that whatever helps his own cause is ethically correct. Most sociologists today would reject Comte's view and argue that viewing altruistic behavior as a violation of the rational choice proposition simply means that one is using the wrong standards for reward and cost; for some altruistic individuals, the satisfaction of serving others, even at personal expense, is a great reward.

# Culture, Socialization, and Social Organization

## Culture

A *culture* is a comprehensive style of living that is developed in a society and maintained from generation to generation. Culture is manifested in a group's traditions, rituals, language, social norms, technology, and economic structures. Broadly speaking, culture is everything that is learned by a member of a particular society, though it may include things that an individual learns but which are never made explicit either in the individual's mind or in his or her social interactions. For this reason, many sociologists feel it is difficult to properly study one's own culture; they suggest that only the unclouded eyes of a foreign observer can perceive a society's most fundamental values.

### Material Culture

A society's *material culture* is the set all of the physical objects that the people of that society have either created or to which they assign cultural meaning. Hence, material culture may include objects like books, jewelry, buildings, and furniture; but it may also include natural areas if those areas are assigned significance by the members of the society. As an example of this latter kind of material culture, a sociologist might point to the Native American society, in which the land itself held immense cultural value. Along with verbal culture, material culture makes up the sum total of what sociologists have at their disposal for study.

### Nonmaterial Culture

*Nonmaterial culture* is all of a society's customs, beliefs, political structures, languages, and ways of using material objects. In the United States, for instance, the emphasis placed on religious freedom and individual liberty might be considered an example of nonmaterial culture. The boundary between material and nonmaterial culture is never altogether clear; how, for instance, should one separate the American flag and what it stands for, namely the idea of freedom? Values and norms, as opposed to the physical things that are used to express values and norms, are what make up a society's nonmaterial culture. Typically, nonmaterial culture is more difficult to change than material culture, and its change is more difficult to observe.

## Values as Used in Sociology

The *values* of a culture are its highest ideals. In the United States, for example, we would say that freedom and equality are two of our most important values. Values are usually very general concepts. They may be complementary, as for example the values of hard work and material success seem to go together. Values are quite fluid, and a major focus of sociology is observing how they change over time. Values may come into conflict with one another, which can create social conflict and disorganization. An example of this is the conflict in mid-twentieth-century America between the values of equal rights and segregation; ultimately, it was clear that only one of these values could remain.

## Sanctions as Used in Sociology

In sociological terms, *sanctions* are any rewards or consequences given to an individual or group to pursue or renounce a certain course of behavior. Sanctions may be positive, as when a reward is promised for something done properly, or negative, as when a punishment is promised for something done improperly. Although the most common use of the word refers to international economic pressures (as in, for instance, the economic restrictions placed on Iraq during the 1990s), all societies place sanctions on their members in order to elicit approved behavior. People who uphold the values and norms of the society are rewarded with preferential treatment from their fellows, while those who transgress can be punished socially, economically, or legally.

## DURKHEIM'S IDEA OF THE TOTEM

A *totem* is any object, whether animate or inanimate, that is worshipped by a group as a representation of itself or its beliefs. Emile Durkheim, in his study of aboriginal religion, became fascinated by the idea of the totem, which led him to advance the notion that a society's religious beliefs were a reaction to the social forces in play there. For instance, according to Durkheim the idea of a Creator stems from every man's inheritance of a pre-formed society; that is to say, every man lives in a society that he did not make, obeys laws that he did not write, speaks a language that he did not invent. Might not, asked Durkheim, he be searching for the answer to this social puzzle when he imagined a creative God?

## SIGNS AND SYMBOLS

A *sign* is something that directly stands for something else, as for example the Rx on a building, which stands for "pharmacy." A *symbol* is anything used to stand for something which it is not, though symbols are generally considered to be more abstract than signs. A language is a set of symbols, since the word "tree" is not actually a tree itself, but a symbol that refers to the idea of a tree or to a specific tree. Similarly, a drawing of a fish is not really a fish, but a symbol that conveys the idea of a fish. A symbol can also be used to refer to an abstract concept, as in the example of the American flag, an article that stands for a number of values like freedom, equality, etc. Sociologists are mainly interested in symbols because they illustrate the value assigned by a society to otherwise worthless things, and the way in which a group of people must agree on meaning to interact effectively.

## SOCIOLOGICAL CONCEPT OF LANGUAGE

When sociologists refer to *language*, they mean any system of verbal and/or written symbols that is organized by grammar and used to communicate complex meanings. Language is crucial to the concept of culture, because it is in language that much of the knowledge and information of a culture is stored and transmitted to future generations. Sociologists who study language are concerned with the reciprocal relation between a society and its language: that is, the way that a society is influenced by its vocabulary and grammatical structures, and vice versa. Sociologists concerned with social action study how language is used to arbitrate and create meaning in social interactions.

## NORMS

*Norms* are specific rules regulating behavior in a culture. Norms may or may not be directly codified in the law of a society, but they are intended to encourage behavior that promotes the society's values. Taking again the example of the United States, one might say that treating men and women equally is a social norm, insofar as equality between the sexes is a value aspired to by our culture. Norms, then, depend on values for their justification, and values depend on norms for their enactment. Norms may vary greatly from society to society, such that the same behavior may be approved or condemned depending on where it is performed. Most of the time, norms are so customary for the members of a society that they are performed automatically.

### *FORMAL NORMS AND INFORMAL NORMS*

Norms may be considered formal or informal, depending on whether they are codified in the laws of the society in which they apply. *Formal norms* are written law; examples of formal norms include the prohibition of murder, the forced payment of taxes, and the sanctity of marriage. *Informal norms*, on the other hand, are unwritten codes of conduct. Examples of informal norms might include the prohibition of spitting in public or the encouragement of deference to women. Typically, a society formalizes the norms which are most important, and for which violators should be punished. Formal norms tend to be much more consistent among different societies than informal norms.

### Social Markers, Laws, and Folkways

A *social marker* is any part of behavior that indicates the identity, character, or way of understanding of a particular group of people. Social markers can be laws, folkways, traditions, or other patterns of behavior. *Laws* are simply social norms that have been made explicit and are enforced by the government. There are plenty of norms, though, that are encoded in law but are also internalized-- the prohibition of murder, for instance. *Folkways* are social norms that have become habitual or traditional in a society. In the United States, we are accustomed to tipping a water or waitress for their service: that this is so ingrained in our daily life makes it an American folkway.

### Cultural Pluralism and Subculture

*Cultural pluralism* exists when multiple distinct cultures exist within the same society after a process of accommodation. These self-contained cultures should not be confused with *subcultures*, which are smaller cultures within a large culture. Subcultures usually have a set of norms and values that are different from those held by the larger society of which they are a member. In the United States, we might consider punk rockers or hippies as subcultures, because they have different values than Americans on the whole, but do not really have a self-sustaining or separate society of their own.

### Countercultures

A *counterculture* is any group whose values and norms challenge and seek to alter the values and norms of the dominant culture in their society. Although the term when used today evokes memories of the 1960s youth rebellion in Western Europe and the United States, earlier countercultural movements include the Bohemians in nineteenth century France, or even the early Christians. Countercultures typically appear at a time when traditional norms and values are felt to no longer be appropriate or helpful in making sense of the world. As in the case of a social movement, a counterculture tends to have more and stronger adherents at the beginning of its life; once the counterculture's norms have been partially co-opted by the larger society, countercultures tend to lose steam.

### Dominant Culture and Ethnocentrism

In any society, the *dominant culture* is the group whose norms, values, and behavior patterns are forced on the rest of the society. Many nations, including the United States, have laws to restrain the dominant culture from extinguishing minority cultures. *Ethnocentrism* describes the tendency to view one's own cultural patterns as superior and to judge all others only as they relate to one's own. This philosophy has been at the root of some of humanity's worst atrocities, including the Holocaust, which was perpetrated by Germans who believed they must maintain the purity of their race, and colonial conquests, in which Western nations brutally imposed their customs on various indigenous peoples.

### Cultural Relativism

*Cultural relativism* is the idea that any particular part of a culture can only be understood in relation to the rest of the culture, and as a product of its context. In large part, cultural relativism is a reaction to *Western ethnocentrism*, or the belief that Western culture is superior to all others. It has had the positive effect of undermining scientists' assumption of the rightness of their assessments, but some critics argue that cultural relativism inevitably leads to the absence of any standards at all, and makes judgment (and hence constructive criticism and progress) impossible. Its proponents counter that the general similarity in moral code between various cultures implies that there is a set of innately human values, and that cultural relativism offers the only approach wherein the sociologist can explore the nature of his or her own assumptions.

### IDEA OF PROGRESS, CULTURAL LAG, AND DIFFUSION

In sociology, the *idea of progress* is the idea that social and technological progress is inevitable. A *cultural lag* is created when a change in one part of society is not immediately followed by corresponding changes in the other parts. A typical example is when new technology brings rapid progress to the day-to-day lives of the citizens, and the religious institutions do not adjust their practices to incorporate it. This typically produces a period of relative inactivity in the society. *Diffusion*, in the context of sociology, is the process by which technological, political, and social innovations spread from one society to another. The process of diffusion is usually accelerated in pluralist societies that are used to a healthy internal debate.

### ACCULTURATION

*Acculturation* is the extensive borrowing of cultural traits by one group from another. Acculturation also can describe the exchange of cultural traits between two cultures that are in close contact for a long period. Acculturation may occur such that the recipient culture incorporates new traits without significantly altering its own culture; an example of this is the acquisition of Chinese linguistic characters into Korean and Japanese language. Of course, acculturation may also have a devastating effect on one of the cultures, as in the savagely unequal exchange between Europeans and Native Americans. Many groups are currently trying to resist the acculturation encouraged by globalization.

### CULTURE SHOCK

*Culture shock* is the feeling of disorientation that a person may feel when he or she encounters cultural values, norms, or practices that are contrary to what he or she is accustomed to encountering. Culture shock may occur when an individual goes to another country, moves to a different environment, or simply encounters something unfamiliar in his or her own culture. Culture shock typically has four phases: the honeymoon, in which the new culture is perceived as good; the shock, in which the individual becomes disoriented; the negotiation, in which the individual labors to make the new culture acceptable to him or herself; and acceptance, in which the positives and negatives of the new culture have been absorbed and reconciled.

### INDEPENDENT INVENTION AS USED IN SOCIOLOGY

When a culture is changed by the spontaneous development of new ideas or methods, it is known as change by *independent invention*. There is certainly a degree of independent invention in every society, although sociologists differ as to the exact definition. Some suggest that what is called invention is usually just a borrowing from more obscure sources. Most agree that invention is most common in pluralist societies, in which diverse cultures are allowed to coexist and interact with one another. The independent invention of the various pieces of industrial equipment, such as the steam engine or the assembly line, is the most significant recent example of this phenomenon.

### CONVERGENT CULTURAL EVOLUTION

When different cultures develop similar cultural traits because they live in similar environments, it is known as *convergent cultural evolution*. For example, societies developed in tropical environments have been shown to have arrived at similar agricultural practices independently. Similarly, cultures that develop in densely-populated areas tend to be different from those that arise in rural areas. For one thing, rural cultures tend to place more emphasis on the strength of the family unit, because there are fewer people readily available to care for the young. In urban culture, there may be more emphasis placed on specialization and division of labor, since the size of the population allows for a diverse market economy.

### AVANT-GARDE AS USED IN SOCIOLOGY

The *avant-garde* ("vanguard" in French) are the artists and writers who experiment with new forms of life and art. The expression is borrowed from military terminology, in which the vanguard is the group of expert soldiers who go ahead of the rest to plan strategy and acquire information. In sociology, the avant-garde is of interest because they chart out new values and norms for their society. There is a certain connotation of snobbery in the term, although it was originally applied to people who were repeatedly unsuccessful in the mainstream art world and so had to strike out on their own. Avant-garde artists have frequently been aligned with progressive political movements, as for example the Beat writers in the United States, who empathized with the African-American struggle for equal rights.

### CULTURAL DETERMINISM

*Cultural determinism* is the assertion that the potential for variation in human societies is unlimited, and that cultural forces can shape human nature into almost any form. Sociologists have claimed dominance for various forces, including linguistic, economic, and religious. Cultural determinism is often manifested as the culture's sense of uniqueness. For example, the ancient Greeks attributed their self-proclaimed superiority to their language, and actually coined the term "barbarian" to describe foreigners (literally, those who made gibberish sounds like "bar-bar"). Even today, many Americans feel that the democratic system has somehow made them unique in history. Max Weber made an argument based on cultural determinism when he suggested that Protestantism had resulted in an especially hardy society.

### CULTURAL GATEKEEPERS

The *cultural gatekeepers* of a society are the people who permit or forbid the introduction of new cultural artifacts into their society. Specifically, cultural gatekeepers are people who have control over the means by which ideas are distributed in a society, and so they get to decide which ideas are distributed. For example, radio executives can decide which new songs will get airtime, and so they in effect control which songs will become a part of the popular culture. Of course, cultural gatekeepers like movie and radio executives, fashion buyers, and editors are subject to the demands of the market, and so they cannot always introduce the things they personally find worthy; instead, cultural gatekeepers often simply mimic elements of the culture that are already popular.

### CULTURAL UNIVERSALS

*Cultural universals* are the elements of culture found in virtually every society. The anthropologist George Murdock once compiled a list of these universals, and it included sports, cooking, courtship, dancing, family, games, language, music, religion, and restrictions on sexual activity. Although these elements appear in every culture, the particular forms in which they emerge are quite various. Most of them have a clear role in perpetuating the society; it is easy to see, for instance, why cooking, courtship, and language should be universal. Sociologists are still debating, however, why it is that more trivial things like sport and music should be found in every society, and what role these things play in the continuation of the social group.

## Multiculturalism

*Multiculturalism* is a set of values and norms that suggest different races in a pluralistic society should learn to understand and appreciate their differences, rather than seek to impose one style of life on other people. The multicultural view emphasizes the inherent dignity in all human groups, and seeks to find ways to harmonize relations without compromising any group's beliefs. The United States attempts to promote multiculturalism by protecting the rights of minority groups to preserve their religious and cultural practices. Some critics of multiculturalism argue that it prevents assimilation and integration, and can thereby lead to social disharmony or an under-performing and economically segregated labor force.

## Middleman Minorities

*Middleman minorities* are racial or ethnic groups that are confined to occupations in the middle level of the social stratification. Groups in this role have a difficult time avoiding conflict with those groups on either side of them. For example, in Europe during the feudal era, Jews were only allowed to hold certain positions, like tax collector or merchant. Consequently, they were frequently attacked by either the nobility or the peasants, or a coalition of both these groups. Indeed, some sociologists have suggested that middleman minorities may have been created in some cases to defuse social tension by offering people a ready scapegoat. The societies of China and India have also featured middleman minorities, with similar results.

## Cultural Division of Labor and the Enclave Economy Theory

When certain racial or ethnic groups within a society tend to be involved in only a limited number of professions, that society is described as having a *cultural division of labor*. *Enclave economy theory* suggests that racial or ethnic groups will achieve greater and faster economic success if they are grouped closely together, because they will have more opportunities to create successful businesses that are unique to their group. These businesses will create chances for members of the group to attain supervisory positions, from which they would normally be excluded. Some critics of this theory suggest, though, that there is a limit to how profitable minority economies can become when they remain so insular.

## Social Evolutionary Theories

Sociological theories that consider how social structures contribute to the long-term survival of a culture are known as *social evolutionary theories*. Much as general evolutionary theory asserts that species will naturally evolve in ways that make them better able to prosper (or else will become extinct), social evolutionary theory maintains that the societies best able to adapt to changing conditions and make use of their environments will be the most successful over time. A rather obvious example of social evolutionary theory is the idea that technologically superior societies, particularly those that are adept at constructing military technology, will be able to impose their will on other societies, and hence will survive for a longer period.

## Using Surveys as an Assessment

Surveys help gather information of any type, regardless of whether or not specific names need to be attached. Surveys are useful in determining how a student feels about the instruction. They may be used to determine the level of knowledge on various issues related to the content that is being studied. This could help provide a baseline of where the students are. Surveys that are similar can then be given at a later time to determine what the students have learned. Surveys are useful in determining how the student feels about what he or she has learned in the class from their point of view. Unlike a standardized test score that shows academic outcomes, a survey can provide a more personal level of knowledge that the student may have gained from the class.

### Collective Goods

*Collective goods* are those things provided to citizens by the modern welfare system. These goods are typically difficult for individuals to buy and sell on their own, because they are either too expensive or difficult to divide up into personal shares. For example, in the United States citizens receive the benefits of a national defense, public transportation, and the work of the various government agencies that regulate the economy. Some sociologists argue that countries that provide a wealth of collective goods actually damage themselves, because they encourage the lower classes to wait for aid rather than working. Others say that providing collective goods mitigates the natural inequalities of capitalism.

### Interest Groups

*Interest groups* are organizations that have been created to influence the political decisions that concern their members. Although the phrase has come to be associated mainly with political action groups, interest groups also include trade unions, business and professional associations, and agricultural groups. Although most Americans feel that interest groups wield too much power in contemporary politics, they are not new to the scene; interest groups have existed since the beginning of the country, in large part because they are an effective means of pooling disparate sources of money and power together to pursue a common goal. One thing that is new, however, is the existence of permanent interest groups, as opposed to those that are centered around one issue or event.

### Primary and Secondary Groups

The distinction between primary and secondary groups refers to the varying levels of intimacy and allegiance felt by the members. A *primary group* is one in which the members feel a strong sense of union with one another; they know each other and have emotional ties. A family is the most obvious example of a primary group, although some organizations and interest groups can, over time, achieve primary status among their members. A *secondary group* is a less intimate social network, in which individuals may pursue some similar goals, but feel less of a sense of communion with other members and are more likely to leave the group. Examples of secondary groups are political parties and trade unions.

### Voluntary and Involuntary Groups

A group may be voluntary or involuntary depending on whether its members have consciously chosen to be a part of the group. *Voluntary groups* have members who are aware of their membership, aware of the nature of the group, and are active in it. Examples of voluntary groups are religious groups (in places where religious observance is not mandatory), service organizations, political parties, trade unions, interest groups, fraternities, and business organizations. An *involuntary group* is one in which the members did not choose to join, and in which the members may not even know that they are a part. Examples of these include states, socio-economic groups, races, and ethnic groups.

### Reference Groups

A *reference group* is any group that an individual or group uses as a basis of comparison for norms, values, or practices. Typically, a subculture will use the larger culture of which it is a part as a reference group. An example of this might be the "hippie" subculture in the United States, which forms most of its values as a reaction to the supposedly materialistic and violent trends in mainstream American culture. However, individuals and groups do not need to be a part of the group they use for reference; sometimes Americans use the citizens of other countries as a reference. Reference groups may be used not only as something to differentiate from, but as something to which an individual or group may aspire.

## Crowds and Mobs

Groups of people may be either considered crowds or mobs by sociologists, depending on their character and behavior. A *crowd* of people is any temporary collection in which the attention of the group is all focused on the same object, and in which people are influenced by one another. Crowds typically use a conventional space, like a town square or a building, for an unusual purpose. A *mob*, on the other hand, is a large crowd in which people are violently agitated and dangerous to themselves and others. Sociologists have long been fascinated by crowd behavior, in part because people often behave quite differently when they are in a crowd than they would alone.

## Acting Crowd, Casual Crowd, Conventional Crowd, and Expressive Crowd

The sociologist Harold Blumer coined a number of phrases to describe the various behaviors of crowds of people. The *acting crowd* is Blumer's phrase for an excited group of people who, spurred by some controversial event, are motivated to act passionately. A *casual crowd*, on the other hand, is any spontaneous assembly of people that all pay attention to the same thing for a while, and then go on their way. A *conventional crowd* is a group of people who have gathered for a particular purpose and behave according to the norms prescribed for such an occasion. A theatre audience is a good example of a conventional crowd. An *expressive crowd* is one in which people feel permitted to act in ways that they would not normally.

## Transitivity

*Transitivity* is a sociological term used to describe a common feature of groups, namely that the relations among members will tend to be balanced and consistent. In other words, in a three-person group, or *triad*, if two members are friends, they will likely be friends with the third person as well. Transitivity in relationships is demonstrated in the taking of sides, as when friends rally behind one another not necessarily out of any just cause, but simply because they are already friends. Conversely, relationships develop intransitivity when different members have different feelings about another member: for instance, when two friends fight and their mutual friends are split in their loyalties. Intransitive groups typically break up very quickly.

## Exploitation

*Exploitation* is the process by which one group takes the things that have been produced by another group. Slavery is a clear example of exploitation, in which the work of the slave is taken from him for nothing by his owner. Many sociologists claim that all class stratifications are based on a policy of exploitation, which magnifies already existing inequalities. Marx, especially, made the case that capitalism allows those in control of the means of production to exploit their laborers. Exploitation does not require an economic basis: one of the central arguments of feminism is that men have long used their dominant position in society to exploit the reproductive assets of women.

## Emergent-Norm Theory

The *emergent-norm theory* speculates that crowds of people will develop new norms to deal with morally ambiguous situations. The proponents of this model assert that most crowds are not controlled by a leader or any central authority, and hence have no established norms. Therefore, any people within the crowd that draw attention through distinctive behavior are establishing the norms of the crowd. An example of this is when a formerly passive crowd becomes violent after a few members begin acting that way. Emergent-norm theory underscores the unpredictability of crowd behavior. Critics of the theory state that no crowd comes together without any norms at all, and that not every member of a crowd entirely gives up his self-control and does what everyone else is doing.

## Dyadic Power and Power Dependency

*Dyadic power* is the ability of each member of a dyad to impose his or her will on the other. In male-female relationships, dyadic power is often closely related to the society's sex ratio. If one gender is much smaller in number than the other, then the individuals of that gender usually have a great deal more power. Within a dyad, the *power dependency* of one member on the other is the degree to which that member is unable to accomplish his or her goals outside of the dyad. As an example, when women are in short supply in a society, men will experience a power dependency in their relations with a woman, because there are fewer chances for them to find romantic happiness elsewhere.

## Group Dynamics

The repeated patterns of social interaction within a certain group are known as *group dynamics*. Sociologists who focus on group dynamics insist that human behavior changes markedly when individuals act as a group, as opposed to when they act alone. According to one generally accepted model of group dynamics, human groups go through four stages: forming (in which members come together and acknowledge their similarities), storming (in which politeness is put aside as the group tries to achieve its goals), norming (in which individuals learn how to work with one another and become more productive), and performing (in which individuals are able to work well together towards a group goal).

## Groupthink

Sociologists define *groupthink* as the willingness of extremely loyal group members to ignore any information that contradicts the beliefs of the group. Such groups are typically dominated by strong leaders and are obsessed with maintaining solidarity. Some of the symptoms of groupthink are the illusions of invulnerability and unanimity, self-censorship by members of the group, unfair shared stereotypes of non-members, and an unquestioned belief in the moral righteousness of the group. Consequently, groups of this kind tend to ignore possible alternatives to their ideas, as well as possible risks of their behavior. Most sociologists agree that the tendency to groupthink is an unhealthy and potentially fatal characteristic of human groups.

## In-Groups, Out-Groups, and Greedy Groups

An *in-group* is the group with which an individual feels most comfortable. An in-group could be an individual's family, peer group, or business associates. An *out-group* is the group of which an individual does not feel a part. It is important to note that individuals can be in the same society with the members of their out-group. Sociologists define a *greedy group* as one that demands total loyalty and commitment from its members. Although this definition of the greedy group immediately brings to mind the examples of religious cults and political fanatics, a greedy group can also be as mundane as a middle-school clique that requires its members to dress and act a certain way, and punishes violators with exile.

## Formal Organization

A *formal* (or rational) *organization* is one that is created to achieve specific goals. A formal organization has explicit rules and strategies that are evaluated and altered depending on their effectiveness. It has a clear chain of command, and clear lines of communication along this hierarchy. A formal organization selects and trains its members. These characteristics of the formal organization may seem rather obvious to contemporary students of sociology, but the formal organization as we know it has only been around for about a century. A great deal of sociological study is currently focused on the workings of formal organizations, partially in an effort to determine the most efficient organizational structures.

## Sociological Approaches to Organizational Behavior

Sociologists have developed a couple of different approaches to considering organizational behavior. When sociologists use the *adaptation model*, they are theorizing that organizations either succeed or fail depending on how well they are able to adjust to their external environment by altering their structures and strategies. When sociologists consider organizational behavior using the *selection model*, they suppose that the external environment decides which organizations will succeed and which will fail. In other words, those organizations best suited to the particular arrangement of circumstances at that time will have the best chance of prosperity. The significant difference between the adaptation and selection models is that the former suggests that organizations control their own destiny, while the latter describes a world in which unknown factors determine their fate.

## Expressive Leadership, Instrumental Leadership, and Cooptation

Sociologists describe leadership as occurring in both the expressive and instrumental forms. *Expressive leadership* attempts to maintain friendly and productive relations between the members of an organization. The purpose of *instrumental leadership* is to direct various group members in the performance of various tasks. Of course most leaders, in business and elsewhere, combine expressive and instrumental leadership. When an individual or organization neutralizes potential enemies by making them a part of their own organization, it is called *cooptation*. Karl Marx described an example of this process: a military contingent assumes control after a popular revolution and, by implementing a few of the citizens' demands, manages to maintain power through co-opting the radicalism of the original revolution.

## Management, Span of Control, and Blau's Administrative Theory

*Management* is the coordination of the work of other people. This can involve supervising the work of the individuals within a division, or supervising the relations between divisions. The *span of control* is the number of subordinates that one manager can reasonably supervise. This number is generally considered to be seven. *Blau's administrative theory* states that the proportion of resources that must be devoted to management is proportional to the size of the organization. Some of the accompanying lessons of Blau's administrative theory are that organizations can become more costly to run as they become larger, and that merging companies together may not be as advantageous as was once thought.

## Bureaucracy and Its Critics

A *bureaucracy* is the administrative system of a large institution. Weber wrote extensively on bureaucracies and considered them the best way to organize groups of people to achieve grand tasks. In his vision, the bureaucratic structure would be characterized by clearly-defined hierarchies and concrete regulations, and would thus be rational and professional. In reality, however, most bureaucracies have suffered from inefficiency, incompetence, and an inability to adapt quickly. One of the most common critiques of the bureaucratic system is known as the *Peter Principle*, which states that individuals in a bureaucracy will be rewarded for competence with promotions until they reach a level at which they are incompetent, where they will remain.

## Parkinson's Law and the Dilbert Principle

*Parkinson's law* is an attempt to explain why bureaucracies are inefficient despite appearing to be busy. It suggests that work will expand to fit the time allowed to it, so that relatively easy tasks may take a long time to complete if no specific deadline is issued. The *Dilbert principle* is a much more recent theory; indeed, it is named after the popular comic strip. It states that the proper strategy for companies is to promote incompetent employees to upper-level management positions, so that they will not have any direct contact with customers. Although both of these theories are satirical exaggerations of management practice, sociologists who study organizational practice admit that they contain a bit of truth.

### Committee (Jury) Organization

One common structure of human organizations is the *committee*, or *jury, organization*. It consists of a group of people who make decisions by consensus or by a vote. Advocates of this organizational structure praise its reliability; one sociologist who studied committee behavior in depth developed a statistical proof that committees make correct decisions more often than individuals. Some critics argue, however, that without established procedural rules a committee often wastes too much time to be worthwhile. One difference between a committee and a jury is that a committee generally has a task to perform after their meeting, whereas a jury is gathered for the sole purpose of making a decision.

### Matrix Organizations

A *matrix organization* typically operates with two different hierarchical structures at once. One hierarchy is functional, in which specialists are hired and controlled by leaders who understand the field. For instance, engineers hired to work on aeronautical design will expect to have a boss who is familiar with their work. In a matrix organization, however, employees also have to answer to an executive boss; that is, a boss who is concerned with the administrative and financial aspects of the organization. Many sociologists have asserted that the matrix model is the only one appropriate to a high-tech business. Some complain, though, that having two different hierarchies slows down the decision-making process and creates operational inefficiency.

### Ecologies as a Type of Organization

One unique and recent way of structuring an organization is the *ecology* structure. In ecology organizations, the parts are treated as autonomous entities that are responsible for their own progress. For example, in the case of an electronics firm, the finance department is responsible for successfully managing investment and payroll; the engineering department has full responsibility for production, etc. If a section of the organization fails to meet its goals, only the members of that section are punished. Conversely, the most successful parts of the business will receive the most benefits. Some commentators have approved this model as a great way to streamline large ventures, but some critics have noted that unsuccessful parts of an ecology organization have the tendency to become dysfunctional and costly.

### Composite Organizations, Chaordic Organizations, and Emergent Structures

A *composite organization* attempts to fit the right organizational model (e.g., hierarchy, committee, ecology, matrix) to the task. The success of a composite organization depends, of course, on the competence of the leader, and so the track record of such organizations is erratic. A *chaordic* (literally, a blending of "chaos" and "order") *organization* mixes all the different organizational structures together in an attempt to encourage organizations to evolve from the traditional models. The arrangements that result are often called *emergent structures*, because they develop as a response to their environment or marketplace. Sociologists that study emergent structures are typically interested in the patterns of their formation, as well as the ability of an organization to function effectively without a defined set of rules.

## Divisional System, Geographical Divisions, and Functional Divisions

The *divisional system* is the separation of an organization into smaller, relatively autonomous parts. This practice is typical in armies, in which troops are organized into small, identical units, each of which contains infantry, artillery, and cavalry. *Geographical divisions* are those caused by dividing an organization into smaller units on the basis of location, and then making those units essentially independent. This was the model generally adopted by large corporations and armies before the advent of instantaneous communication. *Functional divisions* are those that occur when an organization is broken up into small units with specialized functions or activities. An example of this is when a corporation has separate manufacturing, marketing, and purchasing divisions.

## Interlocking Directorships

*Interlocking directorships* are groups of people who are on the boards of directors for multiple corporations. Otherwise known as the *capitalist elite*, the members of these directorships generally have similar characteristics: in the United States, for instance, they are white males with degrees from top business schools. Naturally, these groups have roughly common interests, namely to keep themselves in power and to maximize the amount they are paid for their work. Their preeminent position in the business community makes it possible for them to achieve these goals and thus perpetuate their power. For this reason, there is much less turnover at the top of the social stratification than at the bottom.

## Strategic Management and Vertical Integration

When sociologists consider organizational policy, they are said to be studying *strategic management*. The study of strategic management may either be a study of efficiency (whether things are done the right way) or effectiveness (whether the right things are done). The sociological study of strategic management primarily deals with which organizational structures and practices create the most successful interactions. *Vertical integration* is the inclusion within an organization of the divisions that control the manufacture and distribution of some particular product or service. In other words, a company that practices vertical integration takes into its control more areas of the same production process. An example of vertical integration might be if a shoe company began to produce and distribute socks as well.

## Automation and Its Consequences

*Automation* is when machines are employed to do work formerly done by humans. This is typically done when an industry seeks to have greater worker productivity, but it may have some costly side effects. The work that remains for people after automation is frequently repetitive and mindless. Sociologists studying the phenomenon have observed increased alienation and lowered self-esteem among workers whose jobs have been automated. Also, automation reduces the need for specialization by driving employees out of their previously unique fields; this creates both unhealthy competition for menial jobs, and confusion over social roles among the workers. Unfortunately, the pressures of the capitalist market make it impossible for most businesses to avoid automation.

## Origins and the Major Features of the World Systems Theory

*World systems theory*, developed by the sociologist Immanuel Wallerstein, suggests that the development of a given nation is most influenced by its stature in the global capitalist economy. Wallerstein divides the world into three types of nations: core, semiperipheral, and peripheral, depending on their global influence. One of the most striking assertions of world systems theory is that sociology, political science, and anthropology are all one science. Wallerstein suggested that nations can be stratified just like the individuals in a society, and that they have the same potential for upward and downward mobility. This was somewhat of a rebuke to those sociologists who optimistically suggested that all nations were progressing, whatever their respective speed.

## Core Nations, Peripheral Nations, and Semi-Peripheral Nations

In the world systems theory of Immanuel Wallerstein, nations are core, peripheral, or semi-peripheral. Wallerstein defined the *core nations* as those with diverse economies and stable political systems. The core nations are the most modernized nations, and they dominate international relations. *Peripheral nations* are those that have to import most manufactured goods, and make most of their money exporting unprocessed raw materials and food to the core nations. This livelihood makes peripheral nations dependent on core nations, and they inevitably are forced to adopt economic and social policies that prevent them from modernizing. *Semi-peripheral nations* are those that are more industrialized than peripheral nations but less industrialized than core nations.

## First World, Second World, and Third World

*First World* nations are those that have advanced capitalist economies and are fully industrialized. The former Soviet states, which are slowly developing capitalist economies after having inefficient socialist economies for so long, are classified as *Second World* nations. This term has fallen out of general use, as these nations have slowly become more similar to First World nations. The relatively poor and non-industrialized nations of Latin America, Africa, and Asia, most of which were colonized or involved in other exploitative trade arrangements with the Western empires at one time, are known as the *Third World* nations. Although these nations are far more numerous than those of the First or Second World, they wield much less political power.

## Mass Society Theories

*Mass society theories* were fashionable during the mid-twentieth century as explanations for rising rates of violence, divorce, and substance abuse. In essence, they blame the shift from small, village-based communities to large cities for alienating people from one another and discouraging healthy behavior. As these theories were tested, however, sociologists determined that although it was true that people with few social attachments would be more likely to engage in destructive behavior, the transition from small-town life to life in big cities did not account for this condition. In fact, people residing in cities do not show any more of a tendency to alienation than small-town dwellers. This is especially true in the United States, say sociologists, because of the prevalence of urban organizations that create small communities of like-minded citizens, even in the largest cities.

## Emigration, Immigration, Internal Migration, and Migration Rate

The terms *emigration* and *immigration* describe the movements of people from place to place. *Emigration* is the movement of people from a particular place, while *immigration* is the movement of people to a particular place. People typically emigrate for economic reasons, or to escape a culture that persecutes them for their religious beliefs or ethnicity. *Internal migration* is any movement from one place to another place in the same society. A common example of an internal migration trend is the elderly moving to a warm climate after retirement. The *migration rate* is usually calculated as the number of people who leave a place as compared to those who arrive, per thousand people.

## Socialization

*Socialization* is the process through which individuals born into a society gradually become participating members. This involves learning the culture (including the prevailing social values and norms) and learning to assume the behavior appropriate to a specific societal role. Sociologists usually distinguish between *primary socialization* (in which an infant acquires the rudiments of language), and *secondary socialization* (in which the individual is trained to join a particular social group). Socialization is impossible without the active participation of the society (especially the family, academic, and religious groups). Most sociologists agree that socialization continues in some degree throughout an individual's entire life, though it is most crucial in childhood.

## Chromosomes, Genes, Genotype, and Behavioral Genetics

*Chromosomes* are extremely complicated genetic structures located within the cell nucleus. Chromosomes contain the *genes* of the cell. Genes are encoded with specific instructions, called a *genotype*, for the creation of similar cells. In humans, 23 chromosomes from the father combine with 23 chromosomes from the mother to determine the genetic makeup of the child. *Behavioral genetics* is the scientific field that attempts to attribute the behavior of an organism to its genetics. Sociologists are mainly concerned with the ways in which genetics affect an individual's social interactions. For example, many sociologists contend that entrenched beliefs that have been identified as internalized norms (for instance the prohibition of murder) are actually stored in the genetic code, because they advance the interest of the species.

## Instinct

An *instinct* is any behavioral impulse that occurs in all the members of a society without having been learned. Instincts are to be found in every living species, but when the term is used by sociologists, it refers to impulses in humans to such things as sex and power, both of which may be seen as components of the larger instinct of survival. The sociologists who place an emphasis on instinct in human interaction do so at the expense of social stimuli, and so this position is often quite controversial. Most sociologists agree that instinctive drives can be altered by experience, and for this reason they now generally refer to "instinctual drives" as the initiators of complex, unlearned patterns of behavior.

## Temperament as Used in Sociology

An individual's *temperament* is the behavior pattern he or she was born with. Sociologists note the difference among infants in such categories as activity level, talkativeness, attention span, and fearfulness of strange situations. Of course, an individual's temperament does not remain consistent throughout his or her life; environmental factors will inevitably alter it in one way or another. Still, the phenomenon of temperament is fascinating to sociologists because it implies that humans bring some genetic predispositions to their social interactions. Temperament is often described as a set of possibilities for the individual, the array of different ways they are programmed to interact with the world. Their actual behavior is a sort of compromise reached between temperament and environment.

## Mental Age and Intelligence Quotient

*Mental age* is the amount of knowledge a person has acquired by a given calendar age; for example, a child that has been alive for seven years but has the knowledge base of a nine year-old is considered to have a mental age of nine. Mental age is used to calculate an individual's *intelligence quotient*, or IQ. Intelligence quotient is determined by dividing mental age by calendar age and multiplying the result by a hundred. If, for instance, a person has been alive for ten years but has the mental age of a fifteen year-old, his or her IQ is 150, as 15/10 multiplied by 100 is 150. The average IQ should be 100, the score of an individual with a mental age equal to his or her age in years.

## Four Stages of Cognitive Development as Outlined by Piaget

Piaget noted four stages of cognitive development in children. *Sensorimotor stage* is the period from birth until approximately age 2, during which the infant develops his or her sense organs and learns that objects still exist even when they are out of the visual field. The *preoperational stage* typically lasts from age 2 to age 7, and is marked by the child's increasing ability to imagine the mental lives of others; in other words, to develop sympathy. The *concrete operational stage* generally lasts from age 7 until age 12, as the child develops a number of cognitive structures, including the rule of conservation (the understanding that an object's volume does not decrease if its shape is changed). The final stage is known as the *formal operational stage* and takes place after age 12. In this stage, which not every human goes through, the capacity for abstract thought (the ability to theorize rather than to rely on direct observation for knowledge) is developed.

### Cognitive Structures

*Cognitive structures* are the general rules in the human mind that govern rational thought. Sociologists are concerned with the cognitive structures that affect a person's interactions in society, as for example the ability to communicate through language. Sociologists have determined in this case that the infant brain's ability to construct linguistic systems will be stunted if the child is neglected. With this in mind, sociologists have begun studying various types of social environments to see what their relative effects on linguistic acquisition are, and how acquisition can be improved. A similar line of study involves the cognitive process of face recognition. Sociologists, having observed that recognition skills emerge by about two months, have focused on how this cognitive structure influences the individual's socialization process.

### Gender Socialization

*Gender socialization* is the process through which an individual learns about the various gender roles in his or her society, and subsequently takes one. Sociological research has shown that boys and girls are treated quite differently in most societies; parents encourage their children to act in gender-appropriate ways, and are embarrassed or angry when children display the traits of another gender. Peer pressure also subtly lets children know what clothing and behavior is appropriate to their gender. Studies of American schools during the 1990s showed that teachers generally assigned different tasks to boys and girls. It has also been observed that most children's books and television programs present stereotyped gender roles.

### Class Socialization

Sociologists have determined that there are fundamental differences in the ways children are socialized, depending on their social class. In fact, research has shown that the specific values stressed by parents vary depending on their class. Middle-class parents tend to emphasize responsibility, self-control, and curiosity, whereas working-class parents are more interested in teaching their children manners, neatness, honesty, and obedience. The inference drawn by sociology is that individuals in higher classes tend to place more emphasis on self-direction and obeying internal standards, as opposed to conformity and obeying external standards. There is (controversial) speculation that this difference is the result of working-class parents being so thoroughly involved in slavish work that they come to identify with the ethics of conformity and obedience.

### Racial and Ethnic Socialization

Sociological studies have repeatedly shown that individuals within different racial and ethnic groups are socialized differently, even when they are a part of the same society. Although the phrase *race socialization* is typically used to describe the experience of minorities or underprivileged races, every individual in a multi-racial society undergoes a degree of racial or ethnic socialization. Primary socialization may vary between racial or ethnic groups, depending on the different traditions, values, and norms of those groups. When the individual interacts with the society at large, he or she will confront the various stereotypes of races and ethnic groups as presented by the media. Sociological studies have also confirmed that students of different races receive different treatment at school.

## Charles Horton Cooley and Contributions to Sociology

Charles Horton Cooley (1864-1929) was an American sociologist who focused on the development of the self in society. The idea of the *looking-glass self* was invented by Cooley, who used it to describe the idea of oneself one creates based on the treatment one receives from other members of society. This theory emphasizes the social nature of self-development, suggesting that there is no individual essence that is not influenced by social interaction. For instance, if a person is regularly treated as inferior by his or her society, he or she may begin to believe this to be true. The looking-glass self theory is quite similar to the *labeling theory* of deviance, in which individuals singled out as deviant by a society often live up to that description.

## Mead's Theory of Socialization

G.H. Mead suggested that socialization is the process of learning about social roles and then taking one. A *significant other* is a person that plays an important role in an individual's life. A *generalized other* is an individual's personal impression of what is expected of them by society. This term is most frequently invoked by the sociologists known as *symbolic interactionists*, who say that an individual who imagines what society will think of his or her actions is taking on the perspective of the generalized other. Children, as they are growing up, at first can only think from their own perspective. In time, and partly through role-playing games like "doctor" or "house," they learn to think from the perspective of significant others. Finally, when their sense of identity (and of the identities of others) is well-defined, they can think from the perspective of the generalized other.

## Mead's Concept of Significant Symbols

George Herbert Mead defined *significant symbols* as those words and gestures that an individual must learn in early childhood in order to make social interaction possible. An infant's first attempts at communication are usually aimed at producing a desired response: reaching out to encourage physical contact, crying to indicate hunger, and so on. Mead referred to these actions as significant symbols because they have no inhernet meaning, but are ascribed meaning by the society. In other words, these actions are more significant than others because, out of the whole set of possible words and gestures, they alone create the desired response. This is an example of how individuals conspire to create meaning in a society.

## Sigmund Freud's Theory of Socialization

Sigmund Freud (1856-1939) envisioned socialization as an ongoing struggle between the id, ego, and superego. The ego and the superego, which together try to control the carnal urges of the id, are not with a person at birth; rather, they develop through interaction with others, particularly the parents. As the individual matures, he or she realizes, sometimes subconsciously, that there are more and less successful ways to get what one wants, and that he or she must often take into consideration the behavior of others in order to achieve his or her goals. Although Freud's conception of socialization essentially describes a race of selfish individuals, it does agree with the theories of Cooley and Mead in viewing socialization as a compromise between individual and society.

## Ego, Id, and Superego

Sigmund Freud called the three parts of the human psyche the ego, id, and superego. The *ego* is the practical, realistic part of the mind. It seeks out socially acceptable ways to satisfy the natural drives of the body. The *id* (literally, the "it," because of its non-human characteristics) is an amoral force aimed at achieving physical pleasure. The id is often described as the animal side of the mind.

It is reined in by the *superego*, which Freud defined as the part of the psyche that internalizes societal norms. The superego is often equated with the conscience. Freud's model has often been used in the consideration of socialization. Individuals who are not acceptably socialized are said to have an undeveloped superego, incapable of maintaining the balance in the psyche.

### Primary Socialization

Typically, an individual's *primary socialization* occurs among his or her family. The family is the first mirror a child develops for him or herself, and it is the family's reactions to his or her behavior that form the behavioral habits he or she will take into the society at large. Mothers and fathers typically have complementary ways of relating to children, which provides for a more balanced socialization process. The presence of siblings can give the child some experience in conflict, cooperation, and competition. Generally, though, primary socialization in the family means the child is born into a particular social status, and will absorb a particular set of values, attitudes, and beliefs.

### Secondary Socialization

*Secondary socialization* occurs outside of the family unit: among friends, at school, and in response to media. A child's peer group provides him or her with experience dealing with others of relatively equal status. In this setting, children can take some power in their relationships, and learn about friendship and conflict resolution. Socialization at school is important as well, because it places the child in a subordinate relation to someone other than his or her parent, and prepares him or her for life among bureaucratic, impersonal organizations. Television is probably the most important socializing agent among the mass media: most research shows that it tends to reinforce stereotypes about social roles and norms.

### Anticipatory Socialization, Desocialization, and Resocialization

When an individual begins to alter his or her beliefs or norms because of an expected socialization process, it is known as *anticipatory socialization*. One possible example of anticipatory socialization is a college graduate who, before actually getting a job, adopts the dress and lifestyle of a member of the business community. *Desocialization* is the process of casting off one version of self and one set of values. Desocialization is followed by *resocialization* into another set of values and norms. Sociologists assert that as individuals move through life, taking on and casting off various roles, they are constantly altering the set of values and norms that are most aligned with their status. Therefore, they are constantly engaged in a process of desocialization and resocialization.

### Internalization of Norms

The *internalization of norms* is a sociological expression used to describe the development of conscience. It refers to the condition whereby the members of a society accept the norms of that society as correct, to the point that they no longer even need to think of them explicitly. Internalization is crucial, because it means that the governing authority does not have to make sure individuals are policed at all times. In the United States, for instance, most citizens simply feel that stealing from one's neighbor is wrong; the immorality of theft is a norm that has been fully internalized in the society. Some sociologists have speculated that genetics may be intertwined with the internalization of norms, as many common norms promote survival and successful propagation of the species.

### Differential Socialization, Horizontal Differentiation, and Vertical Differentiation

Sociologists use the expression *differential socialization* to refer to the way different members of the same society may develop markedly different traits, depending on what role their society intends for them to assume later in life. This differentiation can occur in one of two ways. When sociologists are referring to a fundamental difference in the socialization, for instance the different requirements that a society has for doctors and teachers, they call it *horizontal differentiation*. When sociologists are referring to differences in socialization caused by varying social status, for instance the socialization of the wealthy compared to that of the poor, they use the term *vertical differentiation*. Every individual is subject to both kinds of differentiation in his or her socialization.

## Adult Socialization

The process by which adults learn to assume new roles in a society is called *adult socialization*. The concept of adult socialization is relatively new to sociology; previously, following Freud, many sociologists had believed that all personality development took place in childhood. Recently, however, research has shown that individuals must adapt themselves to function in new groups throughout their lives. This is especially true in industrial and post-industrial societies, in which social institutions are diverse. In these societies, an adult may have to accustom him or herself to different cultures at work, in the community, in the military, and at worship. All of these transitions mimic the initial socialization experience.

## Total Institutions and Mortification

*Total institutions* are those that have closed themselves off from the rest of the world, so that the people living within them have almost no knowledge of other ways of life. Typically, life within a total institution is highly organized and controlled by a strong authority. Some examples of total institutions are prisons, army camps, and mental hospitals. Residence in a total institution is extremely damaging to an individual's psyche. According to the sociologist Erving Goffman, individuals who are part of a total institution are gradually desocialized, a scenario he referred to as *mortification*. The process of mortification makes it very difficult for those emerging from total institutions to assimilate into society.

## Feral Children

Children who have been neglected to such a degree that they act as if they had been raised in the wild are called *feral* (literally meaning "untamed"). Sociologists are very interested in feral children because they display human nature as it exists without socialization. For the most part, it is impossible to transform a feral child into a normally functioning member of society; the essential period of infant socialization cannot be reclaimed once it has been missed. Language acquisition is particularly difficult to feral children, and many grow to adulthood without ever sufficiently mastering speech. Many feral children were originally neglected because they were mentally disabled, and thus face additional obstacles to socialization. Sadly, feral children often die quite young.

## Hidden Curriculum

A *hidden curriculum* is a set of informal and implicit rules that a school teaches children in order to help them succeed both academically and socially. Specifically, the hidden curriculum is those rules that a child needs to learn in order to survive outside the family, in a larger social organization. Sociologists frequently cite self-discipline as the foremost element of the hidden curriculum. Students must learn to work quietly, get along well with people they may not like, follow orders from someone else, and tolerate frustration. These skills are essential to becoming productive members of the economic community in later life. When polled, most Americans have supported this idea of the hidden curriculum by asserting that "discipline" should be the primary focus of school.

### Occupational Socialization

*Occupational socialization* is the process through which an organization adjusts the values and norms of a new employee so that they are in line with the rest of the organization. These values and norms include not only the skills relevant to that job, but also the way the office operates and the way to interact with fellow workers. It makes a big difference whether an individual is socialized to an occupation by him or herself, or in a group. If the individual is socialized alone, he or she typically is more dependent on the leaders of the organization than if he or she had been trained in a group. When individuals are trained in a group, though, they often develop norms within that training group that may be at odds with the norms of the organization as a whole.

### Social Interaction and Interaction Theory

*Social interaction* is the process through which individuals influence one another in a society. Sociologists classify a social interaction as occurring in one of four different ways: accidental (unplanned and unlikely to be repeated, for example passing a stranger on the street), repeated (unplanned, but likely to occur occasionally, for instance encountering a neighbor in the street), regular (unplanned, but quite common, like seeing the same waitress at a favorite restaurant), or regulated (planned and arranged by customs or law, for instance attending church or going to work). *Interaction theories* are different approaches used by sociologists to study these interactions. Specifically, sociologists are interested in the ways that behavior changes depending on the type of interaction.

### Cooperation and Accommodation in Sociological Terms

Cooperation and accommodation are two of the ways the members of different cultures interact with one another. *Cooperation* is an agreement between two parties to work together towards a common goal. Typically, cooperation refers to short-term goals that can be pursued without altering beliefs or values. *Accommodation* is an agreement between two conflicting cultures to acknowledge but ignore their differences and try to work together towards common goals instead. Countries that have two or more societies within them, such as Spain or Iraq, are always trying to work out some kind of accommodation, so that positive progress can be made for all the citizens of the nation despite their divergent systems of belief.

### Exchange and Conflict

Exchange and conflict are two of the forms of social interaction. *Exchange* is the transfer among two or more parties of money, goods, or services. In primitive societies, there was little need for exchange, as each social unit (the family, typically) was self-sufficient and did not rely on trade to survive. As the modern economy evolved, however, the gradual division of labor made it necessary for people to interact with each other economically to purchase the things they could not produce. *Conflict* is the clash between individuals or groups, usually caused by differing values or norms, or by the pursuit of a common goal. Many sociologists claim modern society is the result of relentless conflict.

### Assimilation

*Assimilation* is the process whereby individuals are absorbed into a particular society after having been members of a different one. Assimilation can either be voluntary, as in the case of people fleeing religious persecution to a friendly society, or forced, as in the case of some ethnic groups who have been required to observe national customs contrary to their own. The process generally includes learning a new language and a new set of social values and norms. Typically, assimilation is easier for the young and for individuals that are educated and well-traveled. Many critics of the process argue that homogenizing cultures through forced assimilation stifles innovation and productive dialogue within a society.

## DRAMATURGICAL APPROACH

Sociologists are using the *dramaturgical approach* when they consider social interactions in the terms of a theatrical performance. Sociologists who adopt this perspective view human behavior as a staged effort to elicit the desired responses from other people. People inhabit social roles as they would roles on the stage; that is to say, roles are not honest expressions of a person's feelings or personality, but a formula approved by the society for receiving certain rewards. Some sociologists have expanded this view to suggest that human life is a series of partially improvised, partially choreographed skits in which the players assume recognizable roles so that they can deal with one another. In this view, social interaction is a continual process of mediation between the individual's personality and the requirements of the society.

## ROLE

A *role* is a person's particular niche within a society. Every role has a set of expectations and norms that define how the person holding it should behave. For example, in the case of the role of the father, most societies expect that a person will provide economic and material support for the rest of his family. It is quite possible to hold multiple roles at the same time, and indeed to acquire and cast off roles as one moves through life. Culturally acknowledged roles help to provide a society with its basic structure. Much of the trouble resulting from an individual's passage from one culture to another comes from the difficulty in discovering and occupying an accepted role in the new society.

*Role performance* is the way people in a particular role actually behave, as opposed to the way they are expected to behave as holders of that role. *Impression management* is the conscious manipulation of one's role performance. Successful role management requires that an individual has an accurate understanding of his or her role, as well as the expectations society has for him or her. *Studied nonobservance* is the sociological term for when members of a society ignore lapses in one another's role performance in the interest of preserving harmony within the society.

The *role set* is all of the roles associated with any particular status. A college professor, for instance, must by turns be a mentor, expert, friend, and colleague. *Role strain* is the difficulty an individual may have in meeting the social obligations of a role. Most sociologists would say that every individual experiences role strain to some degree, as no person is perfectly suited to any role. *Role exit* is the process of leaving a role that formerly had been integral to the individual's personality. Everyone exits roles throughout their life, for example by leaving behind the role of son when parents die, or by leaving the role of student after graduation. *Role-taking* is the process whereby an individual imagines him or herself in another role, and tries then to understand the meaning of what the other is expressing.

## EXCHANGE THEORY AND THE THEORY OF LOYALTY

*Exchange theory*, along with symbolic interaction theory, is one of the most common approaches to the study of social interaction. Exchange theory mainly focuses on the ways in which people benefit one another through social interactions. An exchange theorist might examine a romantic relationship, for instance, and describe the exchange of love for security, or characterize the relationship between a mother and child as the exchange of joy for sustenance. Many sociologists criticize exchange theory as inaccurate, in that it assumes individuals always know exactly what they will receive in an interaction, and that they view their social lives in such economic terms. The theory of loyalty suggests that people will prefer to reward someone that they know in a social interaction rather than reward a stranger.

## Impression Management and Negotiated Order

*Impression management* is a term coined by the sociologist Erving Goffman to describe the efforts people make to control how other people view them and respond to their behavior. Impression management is not limited to insecure people; indeed, all individuals engage in it to some extent. A *negotiated order* is any definition of a situation that is agreed upon after trying out various actions and modifying them according to the responses of others. For instance, a company might establish certain informal rules for their board meetings, based on the number of people that want to contribute and the expectations of all involved. This procedure can be changed (that is, negotiated) if it is determined that there is a more effective way to work. Humans are always adjusting their plans and programs to suit the needs and desires of others: these are negotiated orders.

## Gemeinschaft and Gesellschaft

*Gemeinschaft* and *gesellschaft* are two terms introduced by the German sociologist Ferdinand Tonnies, who used them to describe the opposing extremes of relationships within a social system. *Gemeinschaft* (community) relations are typical among individuals with a similar culture, and hence are warm, intimate, and cooperative. Tonnies claimed that these relations are found in small, pre-industrial societies. *Gesellschaft* relations, on the other hand, are found among individuals from differing cultures, and therefore are characterized by self-interest and competition. Societies dominated by *gesellschaft* relations are usually industrial, and tend to have a complex division of labor. Tonnies asserted that no society is either all *gemeinschaft* or *gesellschaft*, but that every society contains these relations in varying degrees.

## Social Bonds

In control theory, *social bonds* are the specific links between an individual and a society that minimize deviant behavior. These bonds can be between the individual and the cultural values and norms, between the individual and the social institutions, and between individuals themselves. Emile Durkheim used the concept of social bonds to explain why Protestants were more susceptible to suicide than Catholics: according to him, the powerful institution of the Catholic Church acted as a strong social bond, such that individuals always knew their role. This feeling of being useful and necessary in society contrasted with the feelings of alienation Durkheim observed in some members of the Protestant faiths, which because of their simpler organization had perhaps less of an institutional bond with their adherents.

## Collective Action, Structural Conduciveness, and Precipitating Event

A *collective action* is any response to events or ideas that is shared by a group of people but is not routine. According to the sociologist Neal Smelser, *structural conduciveness* is the degree to which certain elements of a social structure make it easy to create collective action within that society. A society might be said to have great structural conduciveness if its members are all well informed and grouped closely together. A *precipitating event* is any incident that sparks collective action by confirming fears or arousing passions. The acquittal of the police officers charged with beating Rodney King precipitated violent riots in Los Angeles in 1992.

## Dynamic Density

Durkheim created the idea of *dynamic density*, or the frequency with which members of a society interact, to explain the relative prevalence of social change. Dynamic density is increased by three factors: population growth, variety of jobs, and new communication and transportation technology. When dynamic density increases, so does the society's tendency to *organic solidarity*, or social connections that are based on a diverse labor force. Some sociologists have feared that rapid advances in technology would inhibit social interaction by making people unsure of their social roles. The ensuing competition for desirable positions is one of the unpleasant consequences of a society that enjoys a rapidly diversifying job market.

## RELATIVE DEPRIVATION

*Relative deprivation* is the gap between the expectations of the public and the conditions of life as they actually are. For a long time, sociologists assumed that prolonged and gradually worsening poverty was at the root of revolution. Alexis de Tocqueville, though, in his nineteenth-century analysis of American culture, noted that the potential for revolution is greatly magnified when an impoverished population senses a chance for improvement. Relative deprivation can be caused by rising expectations, as in the case of African-Americans who expected more benefits from the Civil Rights Movement and rebelled in the 60s and 70s, or by a diminishment in quality of life for a group that has grown accustomed to prosperity.

## BIOGRAPHICAL AVAILABILITY

*Biographical availability* is the sociologist Doug McAdam's term to describe people who are free of involvements, like jobs and families, which typically would interfere with their participation in a social movement. McAdam studied the people who volunteered in the Civil Rights Movement and determined that the two most consistent attributes for participants were identification with the values of the movement and an open schedule. In part, the notion of biographical availability debunks the idea that college students led the march for equal rights because they were kinder or better informed. This may be somewhat true, but, according to McAdam, they are also a group that has an excess of free time and limited responsibility.

## ATTACHMENTS, INVESTMENTS, INVOLVEMENTS, AND BELIEFS

*Attachments* are bonds formed between individual members of the society, as for instance the love between family members or friends. *Investments* are the material and emotional costs that a person expends in order to make his or her place in a society and, hopefully, secure the future rewards of participation in that society. An example of an investment of this type might be volunteer work in one's community, an activity which, though not always done for one's own reward, helps to create connections within the community and develop a sense of loyalty in the individual. A person's *involvement* in their society is the amount of time they spend engaged in nondeviant activities, and a person's *beliefs* are their ideas about how the members of their society should behave. To the degree that these four social bonds are positive and strong, the individual is unlikely to display deviant behavior.

## FAMILY HISTORY IN READING DIFFICULTIES

Research on reading problems suggests that children whose parents or older siblings have shown reading problems are at greater risk for reading difficulties than those children of otherwise similar backgrounds. Factors identified as family risk factors include family history of reading problems, home literacy environment, verbal interaction, language other than English, nonstandard dialect, and family-based socioeconomic status. Family patterns of reading problems can be attributed to factors that are shared either genetically or environmentally. Most studies of familial incidence diagnose a child with a reading disability using a severity criterion that would identify between 5 to 10 percent of children who have normal intelligence and have had a commonly effective education.

# Social Stratification

## Theory of Ethnic Succession and Index of Dissimilarity

The *theory of ethnic succession* states that ethnic and racial groups will be affected by neighborhood segregation until they are economically equal to other groups. At that point, they will be able to integrate into the society at large. The theory gets its name from the accompanying idea that slum neighborhoods will house a succession of racial or ethnic groups. The *index of dissimilarity* is a measure of the degree to which a given ethnic or racial group lives by itself or among other groups; that is, the degree to which that ethnic or racial group is segregated. The index of dissimilarity compares the ethnic composition of the city as a whole with the ethnic composition within certain neighborhoods of that city.

## Social Stratification

*Stratification*, literally meaning "layering," is the term sociologists use to describe the inequalities of status in a society. Status manifests itself in three ways in a society: in the forms of power, material wealth, and honor. When an individual possesses a large amount of these rewards, he or she is said to be in the upper stratum or class of a society; conversely, an individual without these tokens of status is considered to be of the lower strata. Every society has a slightly different stratification, though most stratifications are institutional: that is, they persist in a society from generation to generation. There is no society on record that does not have some sort of stratification.

## Open and Closed Stratification Systems

A system of social stratification can be either open or closed. An *open stratification system* has few hindrances to social mobility. In such a society, status is mostly based on merit. The United States aspires to be a nation with an open stratification system. A *closed stratification system*, on the other hand, is one in which there are significant obstacles to social mobility, making it very difficult for an individual to alter his or her place in the hierarchy. India's caste system is an excellent example of the closed stratification system: it is extremely difficult for individuals to escape the social position in which they are born. Interestingly, sociologists have discovered that there is typically less anxiety among the members of a closed stratification system, as they have little concern about changing their status for better or worse.

## Social Class

When people are ranked in a society according to status, they are placed into a certain *social class*. Depending on the culture in question, social class is determined by one's family, personal wealth, education, or other achievement. Before Marx, most social commentators outlined class in terms of the power and wealth already attained by a certain group; Marx, however, suggested that true power (and therefore higher class) belongs to those who control the means to create more wealth, and thus remain at the top of the social stratification. Social class takes on a concrete form in India's caste system, in which social position is rigidly determined by birth; other countries, including the United States, have a more fluid idea of class, in which citizens can move up or down depending on their successes or failures.

## Caste System, Markers, and Visibility

A *caste system* is a system of social stratification that uses cultural or racial differences as the basis for assigning status. Although the caste system is most commonly associated with India, the United States in effect had a caste system during its period of racial segregation. *Markers*, which can be either racial or cultural, are clear distinctions between social groups, specifically those that are the basis of assigned status differences. When sociologists refer to *visibility*, they mean the degree to which other members of the society can recognize a particular racial or ethnic group, and the degree to which members of that group can pass as members of the majority. Typically, minorities that can easily pass for being part of the majority are less subject to discrimination because, looking familiar, they arouse fewer feelings of fear in the dominant group.

## Sociological Distinction Between Classes

Sociologists often divide American society into four groups: upper class, middle class, working class, and lower class. The *upper class* consists of individuals who own a great deal of property, and who therefore have a large amount of power in society. The *middle class* is a group of people who own little property, but who derive a good amount of income and prestige from their job. Sociologists often divide this group into the upper and lower middle class. The members of the *working class* hardly ever own any property, and don't hold jobs that attract much wealth or respect. The *lower class* is similar to the working class, except that the members of the lower class never own property and frequently have no job. The members of these bottom two classes have no authority in society.

## Marx's Concept of False Consciousness

According to Marx, an individual has *false consciousness* when he or she belongs to one social class, but mistakenly thinks he or she has common interests with the members of another class. The classic example of false consciousness for Marx is the proletariat's identification with the value system of the bourgeoisie. Workers assume that they are getting ahead through working and earning money, when in actuality they are perpetuating a system that is designed to keep them at the bottom. In fact, according to Marx, one of the signal features of an exploitative system is that it creates a false consciousness in those it exploits, and thus prevents them from ever rebelling.

## Social Status, Ascribed Status, and Achieved Status

A person's *social status* is the amount of honor, wealth, or power associated with his or her position in society. Status can be either ascribed or achieved. *Ascribed status* is the unearned social position of a member of a society. A person typically has a certain ascribed status at birth depending on the social class of his or her family. *Achieved status*, on the other hand, is a social position that a person earns through their behavior in a society. Achieved status is the result of personal merit and success. Although occupation is generally considered to be the most important determinant of status in modern societies, other things, like membership in certain religious or community groups, can be influential as well.

## Status Attainment, Status Attainment Model, and New Structuralism

The theory of status attainment and new structuralism are the two dominant approaches to understanding social inequality. According to *status attainment theory*, inequality is the result of differences in education, wealth, values, and motivation. According to this view, all inequalities are based on differences in ability. A *status attainment model* is the process through which an individual finds his or her place in the social stratification. *New structuralism* disagrees sharply with the status attainment model, arguing that social structures make it impossible for some groups to attain high status, no matter their abilities. For instance, according to new structuralists, the place of women within the labor market puts them at a disadvantage to similarly-qualified men.

## Master Status, Status Set, and Salient Status

An individual's *master status* is the one status determinant (for instance wealth or education) that most influences the individual's social identity. A *status set* is the full range of social positions occupied by a single individual. A schoolteacher, for example, is the leader of his or her classroom, but may not be especially powerful among the school faculty as a whole. Moreover, that same teacher may have the respect of the community, and yet not be especially wealthy. In other words, an individual may occupy a number of different social positions without them necessarily contradicting one another. The *salient status* is whatever aspect of an individual's status dominates a particular situation. For instance, if that teacher is required to testify in court, the jury will be more concerned with his or her long history of service to the community than with his or her bank balance.

## Status Inconsistency and the Status Inconsistency Theory

Sociologists say a person has *status inconsistency* when they have varying degrees of status in different areas. For example, a church official may have great standing in the community without being particularly wealthy; conversely, a wealthy man may have little education and therefore be looked down on by some others. Sociologists who engage in *status inconsistency theory* assume that individuals of inconsistent status will inevitably become frustrated and will, consciously or not, engage in behavior aimed at altering the current social stratification. Such behavior may or may not be considered deviant. According to status inconsistency theory, every individual desires a social stratification in which the superior qualities he or she possesses are considered the most valuable.

## Occupational Prestige

*Occupational prestige* is the respect an individual receives because of his or her occupation. Sociologists sometimes try to measure an occupation's prestige by administering public opinion surveys. One such survey ranked Supreme Court justice as the most prestigious occupation; shoe shiner was listed as the least prestigious. The degrees of occupational prestige meted out to various occupations are consistent throughout the industrialized world, suggesting that the members of each of these societies use the same criteria in judging. The two factors that research has shown are most responsible for occupational prestige are, unsurprisingly, the rate of pay and the amount of training needed; the more prestigious the job, the fewer people are qualified to perform it.

## Authority

*Authority* is any power that the members of a society consider to be legitimate, and which therefore regulates the behavior of others with their permission. For this reason, proper authority should not require coercive force. Most governments use a mixture of authority and coercive force to implement their rules and regulations. Sociologists use different measures to gauge the legitimacy of authority. Some allow that any regime that is not currently being rebelled against must have some authority. However, this measure does not consider the fact that people may not respect a government but still be deterred from rebellion for other reasons (for instance, famine). A more narrow gauge of authority is that it is legitimate so long as the people have the power to make the changes they deem necessary.

## Weber's View on Traditional Authority

Max Weber described *traditional authority* as the power that devolves upon an individual or group because of beliefs and practices that have long been the custom of the society. Individuals typically accept traditional authority; that is, they do not seek it, and it is not given to them for any special merit. The bearers of titles like king, queen, chief, duke, and even father and mother, are likely recipients of traditional authority. Some societies consider traditional authority to be a gift from the gods. In many cases, traditional authority is contingent upon the bearers acting in a certain way. In imperial China, for instance, regimes only lasted so long as their mandate from the gods held out; in this way, traditional authority may be seen as somewhat of a restriction on the behavior of the recipient.

## Legal (Rational) Authority

Max Weber defined *legal* (or *rational*) *authority* as legitimate power derived from a system of clear laws. In the American system of legal authority, power is given to an office, not to the person who holds that office. That is to say, a senator only holds legal authority when he acts in his role as a senator; if he expects to command others in his private life, he will have to rely on his traditional or charismatic authority. This idea points to the limitation of legal authority, namely that it only applies to the business of the appointed office. Legal authority, then, is only given with the consent of the governed, and unlike traditional authority, it may be revoked by the public.

## Race, Ethnic Group, and Intergroup Conflict

Sociologists consider a *race* to be any human group that has some biological characteristics that make it distinct from other human groups. *Ethnic groups*, on the other hand, are simply groups that perceive themselves as having a unique history and culture. Any conflict between races or ethnics groups is called *intergroup conflict*. Most sociologists feel that widespread inbreeding throughout human history has made the biological idea of race a bit moot; rather, they say, the concept of race is important only as it has created opportunities or rationales for dominance and oppression. That is, the perception of a person as belonging to a particular group is much more significant in their life than any genetic advantage or disadvantage.

## Prejudice and Discrimination

A *prejudice* is a negative or malicious attitude toward a particular group. When a person has prejudices against a particular group, he or she ignores the individual qualities of its members, instead assuming that all the members of the group are identical. A widespread prejudice is an obvious reason for a particular group to have a low ascribed status. *Discrimination* is any action taken by a society or by members of that society to deny a certain group the rights that are given to all the other members of that society. Examples of discrimination include giving lower pay for similar work, or denying opportunities for residence or employment to members of a particular group.

## Gender

*Gender* is the set of traits that a society assigns to males and females, specifically those that are not biological. These traits can be a person's way of speaking, appearance, movements, or anything else to which masculinity or femininity is assigned. The *gender roles* of a society are the distinct tasks and behavior patterns that it defines as being appropriate to either men or women. Any superficial but strongly held beliefs about the characteristics of males and females are called *gender stereotypes*. The *gender stratification* of a society is the unequal assignation of rewards based on gender. Gender stratification occurs in the home and the workplace, among other places.

## De Facto and De Jure Segregation

The segregation of any particular races or ethnic groups can be either *de facto* or *de jure*. *De facto segregation* is the separation of two or more groups that results from informal patterns of social behavior. The tendency of various ethnic groups to live in specific neighborhoods, apart from other groups, creates *de facto* segregation. *De facto* segregation has been increasingly observed in America's public school system. *De jure segregation*, on the other hand, is the separation of two or more groups by law. The segregation of blacks and whites in early-twentieth-century America is an obvious example of *de jure* segregation. *De jure* segregation is now illegal in the United States.

### Creeping Credentialism

*Creeping credentialism* occurs when an employer gradually raises his or her requirements for the qualifications of employees. This process has often been cited as a reason that underprivileged groups have a hard time getting into the upper echelons of society: even as they continue to earn newer and better educations and experience, the requirements for employment rise out of their reach. Sociologists suggest that creeping credentialism may occur without it being an explicit policy of the upper class; when more members of a society are able to earn something (a college degree, for example) it becomes incumbent on those who want to stand out to go beyond that achievement (perhaps by earning a graduate degree). The members of the upper class are obviously the best placed to do that.

### Tracking, Magnet Schools, White Flight, and Compensatory Education

*Tracking* is the term for the school practice of grouping children together in classes based on their interests and abilities. Many critics of tracking contend that it inevitably leads to segregation. *Magnet schools* are those that offer specialized training in a particular field, such as technology or the arts, and therefore attract students with similar interests. Such schools typically have high academic standards. *White flight* is the name given to the trend wherein white parents have moved their children from integrated urban schools to private schools that are *de facto* segregated, or to suburbs that are more dominated by whites. When schools offer enrichment programs in an effort to minimize differences between rich and poor students, they are offering *compensatory education.*

### Comparable Worth and the Equal Pay Act of 1963

One of the last battles for feminism worldwide is the battle for wage equality. Women are typically paid less than men for similar work in countries that are poor and dominated by patriarchal religions. In the United States, the Equal Pay Act of 1963 made it illegal for businesses to pay men and women different rates for work requiring the same skill, effort, responsibility, and training. Business organizations that use the idea of *comparable worth* base their pay scale on the degree of skill a job requires, rather than on differences of race or gender. This system is an obvious effort to combat discriminatory inequalities of pay in places where it is illegal.

### Essentialism

*Essentialism* is the way of thinking about a subject that imagines it to be an either/or proposition, and treats of one dimension of a subject as being determinative. For instance, many people tend to think that an individual's homosexuality is the only important thing about them. This kind of thinking can lead both to homophobia, in which individuals are feared because of one aspect of their life, and gay-rights activism, in which some of the participants associate themselves completely with their cause. Most sociologists stress the wide variety of social roles that an individual fills, and caution against narrowing a person's character down to one attribute. Essentialism, they say, may be good for making quick decisions, but it is too blunt an instrument to be trusted with more subtle distinctions.

### Colonialism

Sociologists define *colonialism* as the economic conquest of one nation by another. This economic conquest is usually accompanied by the conquering nation's control of social and political activity within the conquered nation. Colonialism is generally motivated both by greed and by *ethnocentrism*, or the belief that one's culture is superior to all others. Those in support of colonialism argue that it creates an opportunity to develop the economic and political system of the colonized nation, as in the case of pre-Revolutionary War America. Critics counter, however, that colonialism actually inhibits the development of a nation's economy by transferring its wealth back to the colonizing country, and that, moreover, colonization results in damage to a nation's culture.

### Affirmative Action

*Affirmative action* is the preferential treatment given to members of minority groups, in the hopes of making amends for discrimination against these groups in the past. This can include better access to education and gainful employment. Although in the United States the term is generally meant to apply to minority races, when it was first implemented it was meant to apply to any working-class person. Some critics of affirmative action claim that it is insulting to the races it attempts to aid, or that it creates further divisions between groups. Its proponents, however, point to the benefits of a diverse workplace and the fact that many minorities are still actively discriminated against and need whatever legislative help they can get.

### American Dilemma

The sociologist Gunnar Myrdal used the phrase "the American dilemma" to describe the unique paradox of America, which preserved racial segregation while claiming to advance democratic ideals. America had long championed equal opportunity and individual freedom, and yet in 1944, when Myrdal's book *An American Dilemma* was published, explicitly racist legislation was still in effect. Americans dealt with this paradox in several different ways. Some rejected racism and actively worked against it. Others reconciled this problem by arguing that blacks were not fully human, and therefore didn't deserve equal rights. Most sociologists believe that this hateful ideology was not based on an intellectual understanding, but on some perversely internalized norms.

### Feminism

*Feminism* is both the belief that women are equal to men politically, socially, and economically, and the social movement in support of this belief. Feminists are opposed to any kind of stratification on the basis of gender, and believe that there is no biological inferiority in women. Feminists are driven by the idea that the similarities among women should unite them in the struggle to achieve gender equality. The ideology of feminism has appeared throughout human history, but feminism as a powerful social movement began in earnest during the Industrial Revolution. Many sociologists speculate that this was because large-scale migration to cities took women out of their traditional village roles, and forced them to reevaluate their social roles and status. Feminism scored a major victory in earning for women the right to vote in the United States in 1920, and was a major part of the social activism of the 1960s. Today, feminism is a well-established part of academia.

### Elitism, Elitist State, and Power Elite

*Elitism* is the belief that the individuals who through personal merit or innate ability have risen to the top of the stratification system should govern the rest of society. Individuals may be considered members of the elite because of their intelligence, religion, education, or appearance. A certain degree of elitism is not necessarily a bad thing, as it can distribute power to those best able to wield it effectively. If it is overdone, however, elitism can lead to discrimination and oppression. An *elitist state* is one governed by a single group. Elitist states are notorious for repressing and exploiting non-elite citizens. The phrase *power elite*, coined by the American sociologist C. Wright Mills, refers to a core group of government, military, and business leaders who supposedly control the affairs of the United States.

## Allport's Theory of Contact

Allport's *theory of contact* describes the intermingling of different social groups. Presented by the sociologist Gordon Allport in his book *The Nature of Prejudice*, it states that contact between groups will only improve relations if the groups are not competitive with one another and are of close to equal status. In other words, it is foolish to suppose that colonizing a country will improve relations between the two countries involved; instead, it will lead to subjugation and exploitation of one group. Allport's theories were born out by a study of white police officers in America, who generally were prejudiced against blacks unless they were partnered with a black, in which case their common cause diminished their prejudice considerably.

## Functionalist Theory of Stratification and Replacability

A *functionalist theory of stratification* asserts that inequality is inevitable in any society, since roles vary in importance and in degree of difficulty (being a doctor, for example, is more difficult than being a housekeeper). For this reason, and in order to guarantee that the most deserving people will occupy these important roles, the functionalist theory of stratification suggests that the rewards attached to a role should be proportionate to the role's significance in the society. Measuring replaceability is one way sociologists can determine the functional importance of a role. *Replaceability* is the degree to which a particular role can be filled by the holders of another role. A doctor could probably fill in for a housekeeper, for example, while a housekeeper could not assume the role of a doctor. Doctors, then, have a greater functional importance.

## Evolutionary Theory of Stratification and Conflict Theory of Stratification

Two of the theories used by sociologists to explain social stratification are the evolutionary theory and the conflict theory. The *evolutionary theory of stratification* asserts that the constantly expanding store of culture in any society will eventually make it impossible for any one person to possess its entirety, and so specialization of roles will occur of necessity. At this point, inequality among the roles will develop, as some roles will be more highly valued by the society at large. The *conflict theory of stratification* holds that, in any society, individuals will always fight with one another in an attempt to receive the largest share of rewards possible. For this reason, the inequalities in a society will be much larger than those predicted by mere functionalist theory.

## Upward and Downward Mobility

*Upward mobility* is an individual's ability to move up in a society, whereas *downward mobility* refers to the ability of an individual to lose status. The degree to which an individual has mobility in either direction is determined by the rigidity of the class distinctions in his or her society. For the most part, the United States has been an upwardly mobile society, because of the expanding economy and large immigration rate. However, as the country moves from an industrial to a post-industrial economy, many in the lower classes are missing out on the decent manufacturing jobs that used to provide a springboard to more prestigious work for their children. Instead, they are mired in intense competition for low-wage service jobs.

## Social Mobility

*Social mobility*, or the passage of an individual from one social class to another, can occur in several different ways. If individuals change their social class because of a redistribution of the upper and lower classes, it is called *structural mobility*. An example of this is occurring in the United States at present, as more and more low-wage jobs are shifted overseas, and so a larger percentage of the population now holds what have long been considered prestigious jobs. If the status of some people is lowered, thus creating room for upward mobility, it is called *exchange mobility*, also known as *circulation mobility*. When an individual moves either from the top to the bottom of the social stratification, or from the bottom to the top, it is called *long-distance mobility*.

## Horizontal and Vertical Mobility

*Horizontal mobility* is the movement between two social positions of approximately equal prestige. A factory worker who loses his or her job and takes another, slightly different factory job has not really changed his or her wealth, prestige, or power, and so he or she can be said to have moved horizontally. There are more opportunities for horizontal mobility in large societies with a diverse labor force. *Vertical mobility*, on the other hand, refers to either upward or downward movement in the social stratification. If that same factory worker is promoted and becomes a foreman, then he or she has moved up in the social stratification system. The United States has typically been considered an upwardly mobile society, because the expanding economy creates new chances for advancement.

## Intergenerational Mobility

*Intergenerational mobility* is movement in the social stratification that occurs from one generation to another in a family or other social group. Sociological research has suggested that most new immigrant groups in the United States need at least three generations to reach the upper echelons of the stratification system. Many of these groups start out by forming enclave economies, and then entering the mainstream society once they have built up a significant amount of wealth. Unfortunately, recent economic problems, such as the decline in manufacturing jobs, have made it difficult for minorities to leave the inner-city ghettoes and create a better chance at prosperity and upward mobility for their children.

## Allocation Theories

*Allocation theories* assert that the main function of schools is to place students in the stratification system, rather than to train them for a particular job. An example of the way the allocation system works is provided by the public schools. In many districts, an individual must have a teacher's license in order to get a classroom position. Even a person with a doctorate in their subject, for instance, cannot get a job without that license. Allocation theorists have speculated that the function of licensing, then, is not so much to provide teacher training as to weed out individuals who cannot afford the training, or who are opposed to the system of allocation. The licensing process doesn't necessarily make better teachers, they say, but it makes hiring simpler.

## Poverty

The economic state in which a person or group is considered to be in *poverty* is of course relative to the society. The United States calculates the poverty line as the minimum amount of money that families of different sizes need to purchase a nutritionally sufficient diet. This measure assumes that families will spend one-third of their income on food, and is adjusted every year for inflation. The poverty line measure is criticized by some sociologists, who say it unfairly combines chronic underachievers with individuals who have suffered only temporary setbacks. The American poor come from a variety of backgrounds: some are rural laborers, some are individuals affected by alcoholism or mental illness, and some are unemployed factory laborers.

## Working Poor

Many social commentators have declared that poverty exists because some people are lazy or incompetent, or because of factory closings and automation. These opinions, however, ignore the vast number of people working full-time and year-round who remain below the poverty line. In the United States, one reason for the expansion of the group of *working poor* has been the shift in the job market. A great number of manufacturing jobs have gone overseas, and most factory workers are unqualified for the technology-centered jobs that have been created. For this reason, there are too many people competing for menial jobs, which in turn drives down the average wage paid for these jobs. In addition, the purchasing power of the American minimum wage has declined markedly in recent decades.

## Ghetto Poor

One of the main subgroups of the impoverished is the *ghetto poor*: those individuals living in a densely populated inner-city neighborhood dominated by a single racial or ethnic group. One reason why the ghetto poor have remained a fixture of most American cities is that the manufacturing jobs that used to aid upward mobility have gone abroad. Also, sociologists have suggested that in African American ghettoes the migration of successful members to the suburbs has isolated the disadvantaged members. That is, rather than forming enclave economies that could lift up the community as a whole, many ethnic groups have lost their most productive members. Of course, racism has also played a large part in the perpetuation of ghetto poverty.

## Homelessness

Although many people think of homelessness as a relatively new social problem, it has actually always been a part of American society. The primary reason for the recent upswing in homelessness has been poverty caused by unemployment. Another factor, though, has been the increasing unavailability of cheap housing, particularly within urban areas. In the United States, these troubling economic trends were accompanied by administrations that cut funding to the poor and mentally ill. Of course, sociologists try to avoid generalizing when they discuss why more people are living on the streets today; most would agree that homelessness is the result of a series of troubles (alcoholism, unemployment, poor mental and physical health) rather than just one.

## Machismo and Homophobia

*Machismo* is the exhibition of excessive masculinity, characterized by boasting, fighting, and exploiting women. Generally, this attitude holds that men are superior to women, and therefore should have more privileges in society. Machismo is typically associated with conservative ideas about social relations, such as the idea that women should maintain the home, and men should be allowed to pursue extramarital affairs. *Homophobia* is often a companion of machismo. It is the irrational fear and hatred of homosexuals. This can include the fear of being mistaken for a homosexual as well as the fear of the homosexuality of others. Homophobia tends to be greatest in societies in which homosexuality is condemned.

## Categories that Make Socratic Questioning Usable by Teachers

1. Clarifying questions. These questions ask for more information, verification, or clarification of a main idea or point. They result in students building on an opinion, explaining a certain statement, or rephrasing content.
2. Assumption-probing questions. These questions ask for verification, explanation, or clarification of assumptions.
3. Questions probing evidence and reasons. Such questions ask for more examples, reasons for statements, or evidence. They ask if reasons are adequate, how the process led to the belief, or for anything that might cause a change in the student's point of view.
4. Questions about perspectives and points of view. These questions look for a particular viewpoint's alternatives, how others might respond, or compare differences and similarities among points of view.

5. Questions probing consequences and implications. These questions examine implications of what is said and the cause and effect of actions and alternatives.
6. Questions about questions. These break a question into smaller questions or concepts for added evaluation.

### Overcoming the Black-White Achievement Gap

The black-white achievement gap refers to a general difficulty African-American students experience with academic achievement. They consistently perform below non-minority peers in reading, science, and mathematics. The gap has had negative economic and social effects. Some studies have suggested the difference may be caused by cultural linguistic or cultural differences. Good language skills are necessary for reading. Vocabulary skills support reading development in both younger and older readers. African-American children have been shown to have receptive and expressive vocabulary skills that are below those of their age level. But vocabulary breadth can be increased by direct teaching methods. Such teaching methods may act as a start in improving reading for young African-American children and may narrow the so-called gap.

# Deviance and Conformity

## Social Integration, Moral Integration, and Moral Communities

*Social integration* is the degree to which the people in a group have strong attachments to one another. In a well-integrated society, the social bonds (attachments, investments, involvements, beliefs) will be strong. According to Durkheim, societies with good social integration will have fewer suicides and better adjusted citizens. *Moral integration* refers to the level of agreement regarding moral beliefs within a particular group. Again, societies with strong moral integration will be well-organized and peaceful. A *moral community* is any group within which there is general agreement regarding social norms and values, and in which there are strong social attachments between the individuals. The entire United States, since it has its own legal code, could be considered a moral community, although there are many smaller moral communities within it: for instance, schools and religious and community groups.

## Ideology and Ideological Neutrality

An *ideology* is a set of strong beliefs based on a few abstract ideas. Ideologies are used as systems for understanding and responding to world events. Although the word has acquired a negative connotation due to its association with radical religious and political groups, it should be noted that every society has an ideology of some sort. In fact, social critics of the twentieth century have argued that every society has internalized its core ideology to the point that it is never made explicit, and never even considered unless it is challenged. This is a society's *neutral ideology*, and it is the job of the sociologist to root it out and analyze it.

## Social Disorganization

*Social disorganization* is the state of a society in which there is little agreement about fundamental values and norms, and in which there are weak bonds both among individuals and between individuals and social institutions. Early social disorganization theorists speculated that cities were rife with crime and deviance because they were socially disorganized. They focused their attention on slums and inner-city neighborhoods that seemed to have unstable organizations, and were not surprised to discover many social problems. Later research, however, has suggested that early theories of social disorganization mistook poverty for disorganization, and in some cases were guilty of racist condescension. At present, there is considerable debate in sociology as to what exactly constitutes social disorganization.

## Social Problems in the Context of Sociology

*Social problems* are those social conditions that the dominant group deems harmful to society. Social problems typically endure over a long period, during which there is much debate about possible solutions. Contemporary social problems include poverty, obesity, substance abuse, crime, and depletion of natural resources. Sociologists research social problems to determine their causes and assess the efficacy of various solutions. Some sociologists have suggested that social problems like crime, substance abuse, and the depletion of natural resources are the inevitable result of the market economies that currently dominate the United States and Western Europe.

## Durkheim's Concept of Anomie

*Anomie*, a word introduced to sociology by Emile Durkheim, refers to the vague condition of morals in a society when the members have either lost their understanding of the cultural norms or have lost belief in them. This typically occurs when a society undergoes some massive economic change and the old ways of doing things no longer apply. The result is a murky, chaotic society, in which individuals are beset by anxiety, hopelessness, and lack of purpose. Anomie should not be confused with *anarchy*, though the two concepts are closely related. Whereas anarchy is the lack of tangible authority, anomie is a more abstract loss of values and norms.

### Common Theories of Social Disorganization

The early consensus among sociologists regarding social disorganization was that groups with a common set of values and a strong bond to social institutions would be socially organized, and hence would be less prone to deviance. This idea was supported by the research of the Chicago School of sociologists, who observed crime-ridden inner-city neighborhoods and diagnosed the cause as social disorganization. Later theorists tried to associate disorganization with certain environments; specifically, they linked urban industrial areas with high rates of crime. In recent years, however, all the prior conceptions of social disorganization have been criticized heavily, as sociologists have suggested that what appears to be a normless society may in fact be one with several or competing sets of norms.

### Deviance

*Deviance* is any behavior that violates the norms of the society in which it is performed. Deviant behavior should not be confused with unusual behavior; some individuals achieve unprecedented success without being deviant, while drug abuse and petty crime are both deviant and quite common. Deviance is not always negative, however. Sociologists cite a number of positive functions of deviance: it unifies the conforming population, clarifies the social boundaries, and can often be a force for social change. Many of a culture's greatest advances are the result of innovative deviance. It should be stressed, then, that there is no such thing as absolute deviance; instead, what is deviant is simply whatever a society deems to be so at a particular moment in its history.

### Cesare Lombroso

Cesare Lombroso (1835-1909) was an Italian physician who greatly influenced sociology's understanding of deviant behavior. Lombroso asserted that deviant behavior is inherited, and that deviant individuals can be distinguished by their physical characteristics: large jaws, hawk-like noses, fleshy lips. He made great use of statistics and measurements to support his claims, even going so far as to associate specific facial features with specific types of deviant behavior. Though today we would consider Lombroso's work dangerous, if not outright racist, it should be noted that he held a very progressive view of punishment, maintaining throughout his career that deviants could be rehabilitated without strong consequences. Lombroso's theories, which have been entirely discredited, were the basis of the eugenics movement of the early-twentieth century.

### Differential Association Theory, Structural Strain Theory, and White-Collar Crime

Differential association theory and structural strain theory are two sociological attempts to explain deviant behavior. *Differential association theory* links an individual's deviant behavior to his or her interactions with other people who engage in that behavior. In other words, sociologists who assert this theory view deviant behavior as something learned through social interaction. *Structural strain theory*, on the other hand, suggests that deviance is the result of frustration or alienation due to a weak or inferior position in the social structure. One common example of structural strain theory is the assumption that people steal because they are impoverished. Structural strain theory has a difficult time accounting for *white-collar crime* (that is, crimes committed by a person of high social status during the course of his or her business), because the individual has no discernable motive for deviance.

### Labeling Theory, Primary Deviance, and Secondary Deviance

A *labeling theory* attempts to explain deviant behavior as the individual's reaction to being identified within society as a deviant. *Primary deviance* is the act or acts that cause a person to be labeled by society as a deviant, and *secondary deviance* is whatever deviant acts are performed in response to being labeled a deviant. Labeling theory has led to the development of mediation programs, restitution and reparation arrangements, and even victim-offender forgiveness ceremonies. All of these hope to remove the shame and negative self-image from the former deviant. Some critics argue, however, that labeling theory is impractical and unable to properly assess repeated and violent crime.

### Subcultural Deviance and Deviant Role

A person exhibits *subcultural deviance* when he or she violates the prevailing norms of a society while adhering to the norms of a subculture within that society. In the United States, one might use the example of the punk subculture: punks flout the dress and behavior norms of mainstream American society, yet they adhere to a quite stable system of norms among themselves. A *deviant role* is one that has behavioral expectations that violate the values of the society of which it is a part. The proper performance of the role of murderer, for example, clearly contradicts the norms of any society that strives for nonviolence and respect for all its members. Individuals who identify with a deviant role typically have a much harder time reforming than those for whom deviance is not part of self-identity.

### Intentional Deviance, Impulsive Deviance, and Stake in Conformity

Deviant behavior can be described as either intentional or impulsive. *Intentional deviance* is the result of a rational decision-making process. Such planned deviance is typically performed for reasons that make sense to the individual, and therefore is typically performed over a longer period than is *impulsive deviance*, which is deviant behavior stemming from some wild emotional state or personal trauma. Whereas most burglaries are acts of intentional deviance, most homicides are acts of impulsive deviance carried out in a moment of passion. An individual's *stake in conformity* is the set of things he or she could potentially lose if caught engaging in deviant behavior. These are the things a person protects by adhering to the prevailing social norms.

### Forms of Self-Annihilation

Emile Durkheim, in his large body of work on suicide, distinguished between several forms of self-annihilation. *Altruistic suicide* is caused by an extreme commitment to a group or community. A contemporary example is Muslim suicide bombers, who destroy themselves because of their intense devotion to an extreme version of Islam. A suicide that results from a lack of social norms, or anomie, is referred to by Durkheim as an *anomic suicide*. An *egoistic suicide* is caused by social isolation or excessive devotion to the self. A *fatalistic suicide* occurs when a person takes his or her own life in order to evade what appears to them to be a dismal future.

### Social Control

*Social control* is a society's efforts to maintain conformity to the norms. *Informal social control* is exercised when an individual is pressured by other individuals to adhere to the social norms. When the expectations of a larger group influence the behavior of an individual, he or she is said to be experiencing *group pressure*. Informal social controls can be exercised in almost any setting, though individuals tend to be most influenced by the pressure from their religious, academic, and family groups. *Formal social control* is exercised by social organizations that exist specifically to maintain respect for the norms. This category includes everything from laws and government structure to the police force created to enforce the laws.

## Capital Punishment and Other Forms of Social Control

Prevention and deterrence are two strategies of social control. *Prevention* is the attempt by a society to eliminate either the opportunity for deviant behavior or its causes. *Deterrence*, on the other hand, is the use of punishment (or the threat of punishment) to remove the desire of individuals to engage in deviant behavior. *Capital punishment* (the death penalty) is intended to be a strong deterrent against crime, though its effectiveness in this regard has been frequently challenged. Because most crimes punishable by the death penalty are instances of impulsive deviance (that is, crimes of passion), critics contend that the threat of capital punishment will not enter the mind of the offender.

## Deterrence Theory

*Deterrence theory* suggests that immediate and severe punishment will diminish the frequency of a crime. Most legal systems, including that of the United States, currently operate according to the theory of deterrence rather than prevention. One obvious example of deterrence theory in practice is the arms race between the United States and Soviet Union during the Cold War. Both sides hoped to prevent a devastating nuclear war by building up their own arsenal, and thereby dissuading the other side from attacking. Though catastrophic deviance was avoided, the financial and emotional cost of this policy was extremely high. Sociologists note that deterrence theory, while perhaps a viable method of decreasing deviance, does not consider the motives for deviance.

## Control Theory

Sociologists use *control theory* to explain the relative prevalence of deviance in various societies. Basically, control theory suggests that societies in which the individual feels a strong bond with his or her community will contain fewer incidents of deviant behavior, while societies in which individuals feel alienated from their fellows will be more prone to deviance. The manner in which a society maintains these bonds can be either formal or informal. *Formal social controls* are embodied in explicit laws and rules, whereby deviance is punished. *Informal social controls* are typically less obvious; they consist of the connections that a society allows to be made among people in religious or other community groups. When informal social controls are strong, formal controls are much less necessary.

# Social Institutions

## Society and Nation as Used in Sociology

A *society* is an independent and self-supporting group of individuals. These individuals are united by social relationships, and are set apart from other societies by boundaries that are clear to the members of that society. Also, societies tend to have a specific geographical territory, and to endure for a significant period of time. Although the concepts *society* and *nation* are often lumped together in expressions like "American society," these terms are not synonymous. On the contrary, it is quite possible for several societies to exist within a single nation (as in the various warring factions within modern Iraq), as well as for more than one nation to contain members of a single society (as in the case of North and South Korea or, formerly, East and West Germany).

## Utopian and Anarchist as Used in Sociology

Utopians and anarchists both have extreme conceptions of an ideal society. A *utopian* is one who envisions a perfect society (known as a utopia). Typically, utopian schemes are not meant to be enacted, but are created in order to illustrate the ills of society. An *anarchist* has a much more pragmatic program: he believes that government is essentially unjust and hostile to human nature. For this reason, anarchists have proposed through a variety of means to destroy political institutions and establish a society without laws or government. Though anarchism may sound destructive, at its heart is a sincere belief in the worth of individual freedom and the inherent goodness of most people.

## Social Structure

The *social structure* of a society is defined by any characteristic of that society, as distinguished from characteristics of the individuals that compose it. In other words, the social structure is not determined by the people in a society, but by the systems in which they interact with each other and with the values of the society. Sociologists divide social structures into four categories: normative (the relationship between people and social norms), ideal (the relationship between the people and the society's belief system), interest (the relationship between the people and their desires), and interaction (the relationships between people). Sociologists study these relationships to discover how people of different classes relate to social structures, as well as to determine how the structures themselves contribute to the quality of life.

## Family as a Sociological Concept

Sociologists generally consider the *family*, a small social group organized by the idea of kinship, to be the basic unit of society. The size and configuration of the family vary from culture to culture, but the general functions remain the same. The most obvious and important function of the family is to nurture and socialize the young, but the stability provided by family life is also a benefit to the society at large. Sociologists often trace the history of a given society through a study of its families. In the United States, for instance, family structure was extremely rigid and stable during the colonial period, as adverse economic conditions made family members very dependent on each other. As the country became more prosperous, however, family life became more and more improvised and careless, resulting in a rise in crime. In the early eighteenth century, however, what we think of as the traditional family roles (that is, father as breadwinner, mother as caretaker) appeared, and family structure became much more stable.

## Marriage and Conjugal Career as Used in Sociology

In sociological terms, a *marriage* is a formal commitment between individuals to maintain a long-term relationship, which traditionally have been between a heterosexual man and a heterosexual woman. The marital relationship entails specific rights for each member, as well as specific duties, often including the responsibility of raising children together. Indeed, many sociologists have speculated that the institution of marriage developed as a means of providing a stable social structure in which children could be nurtured and socialized. Many sociologists claim that the overall stability of a society is indicated by the stability of its marriages. An individual's *conjugal career* is his or her history of marriage.

## Endogamy, Exogamy, Polygamy, Polyandry, and Polygyny

Sociologists make several distinctions within the institution of marriage, to indicate differences in arrangement and configuration. *Endogamy* is the practice of forcing someone to marry within his or her own group. The group in question could be the individual's religious, tribal, racial, national, or other group. *Exogamy*, on the other hand, is the practice of marrying outside the group. *Polygamy* describes any marital group that consists of one man or woman and his or her multiple spouses. Within polygamy, *polyandry* is the formation of marital groups consisting of one wife and two or more husbands. *Polygyny*, on the other hand, is the formation of marital groups of one man and two or more wives.

## Patrilineal, Matrilineal, Patrilocal Rule of Residence, and Matrilocal Rule of Residence

In a society operating on the principle of *patrilineality*, a person inherits his or her title and property from his or her father's side of the family. Patrilineal descent is much more common than *matrilineal descent*, in which things are inherited from the mother's side. In fact, societies that operate on matrilineality often transfer property not to the women themselves, but to the male heirs of the woman. For this reason, even in such a female-centered system, women see little material benefit. In a society operating on a *patrilocal rule of residence*, married couples will live either with or close to the man's family. In a society observing a *matrilocal rule of residence*, married couples will live with or near the woman's family.

## Incest Taboo

The *incest taboo* is the prohibition of sexual relations between certain members of the same family. This prohibition exists in almost all human societies. Indeed, sociobiologists (those sociologists who study how humans may have genetically evolved some of their social tendencies) point to the incest taboo as one of the great examples of a trait that has evolved through human history. Because babies born from incest are at a greater risk of birth defects, they say, natural selection has tended to eliminate those who practice it from the species. Over thousands and thousands of generations, the incest taboo has developed in almost every society in the world.

## Religion and Its Treatment in Sociology

According to sociology, a *religion* is a socially organized system of beliefs and practices having to do with questions about the meaning of life. Religions typically assume the existence of the *supernatural*, or that which is beyond the scope of natural law. Some commentators extend the definition to say that religion is concerned with giving people the hope of future rewards which they will not be able to obtain in this life. Religions are distinguished by their particular beliefs, practices, and symbols. Sociologists are mainly concerned not with the validity of any religious beliefs, but with the ways that religious groups form and interact both among themselves, and with the society at large.

### Religious Economy

A society's *religious economy* is its set of competing religious faiths, including their adherents. Though many societies claim to have only one religion, this is never true; always, there are competing versions of the faith, as well as pressures toward secularization that cause splinters within the religion. The American religious economy is very diverse, and is characterized by a lack of government interference. Though attendance at religious programs is high, most religious groups in the United States have become secularized, a process which is unsatisfying to many devout believers. For this reason, the various revival movements also have a wide following in America. Even among non-churchgoers, the belief in God and in supernatural forces in general is very high in the United States.

### Civil Religion and Invisible Religion

According to Bellah, a *civil religion* is one that justifies the conduct of a nation by suggesting that God has specially approved that nation's customs and beliefs. The Hebrews, for example, considered themselves to be God's "chosen people"; later, the Western empires imagined that they were doing God's work by converting the peoples they subjugated to Christianity. *Invisible religion* is the idea that religious experience is personal and subjective, and that it cannot be controlled or described by group activity. The idea of invisible religion usually is more popular in secular societies where religious institutions have entered fully into public affairs and left behind their focus on personal questions of existence.

### Fundamentalism, Animism, Theism, and Evangelicals

When sociologists refer to *fundamentalism* in the context of any religion, they mean a movement to eschew the corruption and decadence of modern society and return to the purity of the religion's basic values. *Animism* is the idea that all of the physical objects in the world, both alive and dead, are animated by active spirits. These spirits typically pursue their own interests as part of some supernatural community. *Theism*, on the other hand, is the doctrine that credits the supernatural with creating all of the events and objects of the world. Christianity is a form of theism. Those Christians who feel compelled to make converts to the gospel are called evangelicals.

### Religious Pluralism, Religious Innovation, and Revival

When the same society contains several religions, that society is said to display *religious pluralism*. The United States is a good example of a nation with several religions, which for the most part exist in peace with one another. Any time a new religion appears in a society, whether spontaneously or as an import from another culture, the process is called *religious innovation*. The work of Jesus Christ, then, is a case of religious innovation, as was the colonial effort to convert the Chinese to Christianity. When sociologists refer to a *revival*, they mean a movement within a religious organization that breaks away from the main body and seeks to reestablish an older, less secularized version of the faith. Revivals typically focus on the mystical, supernatural aspects of a religious faith.

### Church, Sect, Sect Formation, and Church-Sect Theory

In sociology, a *church* is a religious body that exists in a low state of tension with the surrounding society. By contrast, a *sect* is a religious body that exists in a high state of tension with the rest of society. Nevertheless, sects by definition remain within the normal religious conventions of their society. When a group splinters off from the body of a larger religious organization and moves into a state of higher tension with the society at larger, sociologists call the process *sect formation*. *Church-sect theory* is the proposition that, in time, successful sects will become churches; that is, either they or the surrounding society will evolve so that there is less tension between them. Once this process is complete, the stage will be set for the creation of new sects. This cycle is continual.

## Charisma, Cults, and Cult Formation

When sociologists refer to *charisma* in the context of religion, they are referring to the ability of some religious leaders to influence their followers. *Cults* are movements supporting forms of religion that are either new or untraditional for the society in which they take place. Some recent cults in the United States include the Branch Davidians, a radical offshoot of Christianity, and the Heaven's Gate cult, a group that believed the end of the world was presaged by the Hale-Bopp comet. *Cult formation* is the process whereby those claiming to have new revelations are able to assemble a group of followers. Typically, the original members of a cult are drawn in by the personal charisma of some leader, or by their genuine belief in the tenets of the cult. Later members may be drawn in only by their desire to be a part of a group.

## Secularization and Secularism

*Secularization* is the process by which religious organizations become more involved in the mundane affairs of the community, and consequently provide a less mystical version of divinity. It is usually preceded by a society's emphasis on science and rationality as the basis for making political and economic decisions. When this occurs, clergy members often feel they must enter into the public arena more often in order to remain relevant. This, in turn, has the effect of trivializing religion for many people, and giving rise to fundamentalist movements. In secularized societies, religious faith is a personal choice rather than an internalized part of the community. Secularization should not be confused with *secularism*, which is the philosophical argument that societies will be better off if they abandon religion in political and economic matters.

## Weber's Conception of the Protestant Ethic and the Spirit of Capitalism

According to Weber, the *Protestant ethic* is a set of doctrines asserting that economic success is a reflection of the grace of God. These doctrines are based mainly on passages from the Old Testament, for instance when God commands Adam to "cultivate and keep" the Garden of Eden. Protestants extended the idea of the spiritual vocation to include their more worldly work, and considered toil to be somehow spiritually purifying. The *spirit of capitalism*, said Weber, is the secular version of the Protestant ethic. He defined it as a system of values including industry and thrift. Interestingly, Weber himself was not enamored of this ideology; he claimed that it made people into mindless drudges, and robbed life of its joy.

## State as Used in Sociological Terms

In sociological terms, the *state* (or government) is the organized monopoly on the use of coercive force within a society. A state has defined borders and usually enjoys some sort of autonomy. The responsibilities of the state are usually to protect property rights and facilitate the economic exchange that sustains the society. In sociological theory, there have been two main approaches to considering the origin and nature of the state. One view, proposed by John Locke, among others, was that the state forms at the discretion of the people in it, who have the authority to alter its configuration if it no longer meets their needs. In this view, the state operates with "the consent of the governed." Karl Marx, however, disagreed with this notion: he claimed that the state was the apparatus whereby the dominant group exploited the lower classes, who had no authority whatsoever.

## Civil Society

The phrase *civil society* refers to the social organizations and institutions that are not a part of the state apparatus, and so do not have the authority to use coercive force. Civil society institutions may include civic clubs, trade unions, the media, charities, volunteer organizations, religious groups, or academic organizations. Some countries, of course, do not have a civil society, because all of the institutions are in some fashion controlled by the state. In most places, though, the civil society is primarily motivated to develop the society and promote the public interest. Many contemporary sociologists argue that the institutions of the civil society are under siege by the forces of globalization, which they say will eradicate local institutions.

## Welfare State

A *welfare state* provides services like education, housing, health care, and social security to the public. The welfare state evolved gradually during the late-nineteenth and twentieth centuries, as wealthy Western governments began to feel pressured to extend humanitarian benefits to impoverished members of the community. This trend was accelerated by the Great Depression. Today, supporters of the welfare state claim that the government has not only an ethical obligation to aid its citizens, but that this policy will encourage a productive labor force. Critics counter that welfare states create lazy people, and that the potential for innovation and great prosperity in a capitalist market can only be achieved by individuals motivated by self-interest.

## Oligarchy and the Iron Law of Oligarchy

*Oligarchy* is rule by only a few individuals or organizations. The *iron law of oligarchy*, as devised by the sociologist Robert Michels, is the sequence of events that leads to power being controlled by only a few people. Michels claimed that this almost always happens as organizations become larger and more complex. First, leadership positions are assumed by those with administrative or public relations skills. Soon, this group becomes greedy and unwilling to tolerate any challenges to its authority. Finally, the group safeguards its power by implementing conservative rules in the organizations (life-time appointments, for instance). One of the key features of the iron law of oligarchy is that it implies that power will become vested in a few people for structural reasons, not because of their particular merit.

## Communism

According to Marx, *communism* is the state of a classless society, in which the absence of inequalities has made the government obsolete. According to Marx, this state would occur when the *proletariat*, or working class, overthrew their bourgeois masters. In a communist state, property is owned by the community and capital is divided equitably. Communism is distinguished from socialism in that it arises after a revolution, rather than as the crowning phase of a long social transition. The communism that appeared in the Soviet Union after the Russian Revolution of 1917 never fully realized the spirit of Marx, since a massive and greedy bureaucracy controlled production and distributed benefits unfairly. Most states that still purport to be communist (for instance China and Cuba) are gradually moving towards a more free market approach.

## Spoils System

A *spoils system* is one in which the winners of an election take over all the government jobs. This process has existed in American politics since its creation, and has forebears in past monarchies. The problem with the spoils system is that it means every new administration will be filled with novices, many of whom are likely to be incompetent. It also makes it impossible for individuals to have lifelong careers in government (though this may not be such a bad thing for the society at large). In the United States, the government has tried to solve the problems created by the spoils system by instituting a Civil Service exam, so that government hiring and promotion might be based more often on merit than favoritism.

## Totalitarianism

*Totalitarianism* is a political system in which the government controls most aspects of the lives of individuals, and dissension or the free discussion of ideas is not tolerated. Totalitarian regimes typically have an ideology that encompasses all parts of social life, and some kind of organization (or political party) for maintaining control. This organization is led by a dictator, who demands total subservience from his citizens. For a long time, scholars assumed that the Nazi and Soviet states functioned in this way, though later research has uncovered a host of inefficiencies and internal debate. Totalitarian regimes generally emerge from states of chaos, in which a confused and disoriented public will embrace any coherent ideology.

## Capitalism

*Capitalism* is an economic system that emphasizes exchange within a free market and strongly supports individual property rights. In theory, capitalism allows any citizen to benefit him or herself by increasing efficiency. Typically, the means of production are owned almost entirely by private interests, and operated for the profit of the owners. The role of the government is simply to protect property rights and make sure that trade is conducted fairly. Some proponents of capitalism, however, claim that any government interference is damaging to the market, and that for this reason there has never been an instance of pure capitalism. Sociologists and economists are split as to whether capitalist economies tend to enrich or impoverish more people.

## Oligopoly

When an industry is controlled by a small number of very large businesses, it is said to be an *oligopoly*. In the United States, over half of the distinct industries are controlled by oligopolies. These groups are able to stifle competition by buying up resources or by temporarily cutting prices, strategies which are impossible for smaller companies. In this way, oligopolies tend to quash innovation and keep power in the hands of conservative corporations. The power accrued by the members of an oligopoly also gives them the license to make decisions which may be healthy for them but destructive to the society as a whole. The automotive industry's reluctance to pursue economy cars cost millions of American their livelihoods when Japanese manufacturers dominated the 1970s and 80s.

## Socialism

*Socialism* is a political system that attempts to eliminate the vicious competitiveness of capitalism, in favor of a social structure based on cooperation and equality. Socialists seek to establish an economy that works for the good of all members of the society, not just the members of a privileged class. Typically, is accomplished by taking the control over the means of production from the bourgeoisie and returning it to the workers (proletariat) themselves. Socialism in practice has had mixed results: although some of the socialist reforms in Western Europe, for instance the nationalization of some industries, have been successes, the full-scale implementation of socialism in the Soviet Union and other Eastern European countries never realized the visions of its architects.

## Unions

*Unions* are occupational organizations that work to advance the interests of their members by raising wages, guaranteeing their members the exclusive right to perform certain tasks, and improving working conditions. The trade union is a good modern example of a *coalition*, a joining of weaker parties to oppose a strong power. Unions can be either horizontal or vertical: a *horizontal union* is comprised of individuals with a common trade (plumbers or electricians, for example); a *vertical union* is composed of all the employees of a certain organization (Wal-Mart or

Delta Airlines, perhaps). Trade unions usually try to get their demands through the threat of a *strike*, or organized work stoppage. Some sociologists say that trade unions arose during the Industrial Revolution, while others claim that unions have existed all the way back to the medieval guild system.

### COMMAND ECONOMY

A *command economy* is one in which property rights are not ensured by the state, and much of the production is based on forced labor. This type of system is also known as a *planned economy*, since most economic activity is planned and controlled by some central administration. The former Soviet Union is a good example of a nation with a command economy; Soviet officials maintained that they could best decide the way to use natural and human resources, and that the economy could flourish if they controlled the way people used their money (that is, by encouraging investment at some times, spending at others). Of course, it has since been shown that it is very difficult for a central authority to accurately gauge public needs, as evidenced by the large-scale famines in the Soviet Union.

### INFORMAL SECTOR

The *informal sector* is classified as all the economic activity that occurs outside the view of the government and typical employer/ employee relations. Trade in the informal sector is mainly conducted through bartering and cash transactions. In the United States, the informal sector makes up only a small part of the total economy, but in less-developed countries it is often a much larger proportion of economic activity. This is because entry into that informal sector does not require large amounts of capital or formal education; indeed, many of the participants in the American informal sector are illegal immigrants who are unable to pursue taxable work. The *black market*, in which contraband is sold and unlicensed services are provided, is a part of the informal sector.

### NUCLEAR FAMILY AND EXTENDED FAMILY

A nuclear family is a family group consisting of one adult couple (one male and one female) and their children. The strong bond among the members of a nuclear family is a consistent feature of almost every society, with one notable exception being the Israeli kibbutz, in which children are raised by the entire community without any particular parents. An extended family consists of more than one adult couple, often the parents, brothers and sisters of a particular heterosexual couple. In many human societies, people live among their extended families, rather than just in a nuclear family unit. This is especially typical in societies where people do not have to move particularly quickly (that is, in agrarian or industrial rather than hunting and gathering societies).

### RECOVERY FROM ALCOHOLISM

Defeating alcoholism is often the most difficult challenge an individual will face in his or her lifetime. Relapse into drinking is common; some studies estimate that 90% of recovering alcoholics will drink again within a year after quitting. The people who tend to be successful at abstaining are those who have something to lose: that is, parents of children and people with important jobs. Almost every recovering alcoholic will experience mood swings and an occasional temptation to drink. More and more, relapse prevention is a part of treatment. Relapse prevention involves giving the individual the information and skills to cope with the temptations of alcohol, as well as providing a support network that the individual can rely on in times of stress. Exercise and a general reduction in stress seem to be the most helpful treatment techniques for creating a permanent life away from alcohol.

## Unrealistic Expectations as a Common Marital Difficulty

However ideal the beginning of a marriage may be, eventually there will be some conflict. One of the major causes of marital discord is the harboring of unrealistic expectation by one or more of the parties. Sometimes, people assume that their partner will always be just the same, physically and mentally, as they were during the period of courtship. They assume that in order to be meant for one another, they should automatically agree on every subject. Of course, both of these assumptions are dangerous for a relationship. In a truly healthy relationship, both parties have room to grow and change without alienating the other, and both feel empowered to speak their minds and to disagree without endangering the union.

## Climate Change

Of all the environmental concerns, global warming is the one that could have the most effect on personal health. Most scientists agree that the massive burning of fossil fuels such as oil and gas are creating a buildup of carbon dioxide, methane, and nitrous dioxide in the atmosphere. This is known as the greenhouse effect, and it is credited already with causing shifts in the global climate. If glaciers continue to melt and raise the sea level worldwide, there could be major problems for man and the many animal species on which we depend. Along with the problems stemming from global warming are those cause by damage to the earth's ozone layer. Scientists believe that the ozone layer, which helps protect life on earth from the damaging radiation of the sun, has been seriously compromised by the release of man-made chemicals called chlorofluorocarbons.

## Social Institutions

*Social institutions* are enduring systems of roles, organizations, customs, and activities that are arranged in a society for the performance of certain tasks necessary to the society. A major part of any society's social structure is its social institutions. Some typical examples of social institutions that are found in some degree in every society are the family, religion, economy, political systems, and education systems. Max Weber believed that a society will evolve institutions of greater and greater complexity until it arrives at the most rational form of organization: the bureaucracy. Later sociologists have discredited this idea both by their critiques of bureaucracy, and by their undermining of the idea that societies always progress positively.

## Baby Boom and Birth Cohorts

A *baby boom* is a brief period of high fertility. Such a period was enjoyed by many of the Western industrial nations immediately after World War II. A *birth cohort* is the group of people born during a certain year or small group of years. A baby boom results in a large birth cohort. Large birth cohorts can cause problems for many areas of a society's infrastructure, from food and water to housing and education. The United States, of course, is now confronting the dilemma of how to care for the baby boomers who are now retiring. Israel experienced a similar population upsurge when the tide of immigrants from the former Soviet Union arrived and began producing children.

## Underdevelopment

*Underdevelopment* in a nation means that it does not have the industrial, social, or political strength that is required to be a self-sustaining party in the global economy. Third World countries that do not have the modern economic conditions possessed by the wealthier nations are said to suffer from underdevelopment. In some countries, underdevelopment is clearly the result of dysfunctional politics; Third World nations are more likely to be ruled by a small group or by a dictator. Underdeveloped nations are typically those that were colonized at one time. Because their economy during the colonial period was so heavily based on exporting raw materials, they never created a manufacturing base and found themselves unequipped for independence.

Sociologists are at odds as to whether First World nations should aid underdeveloped countries by funneling money to them, or by helping them to develop modern economies.

## Representative Democracy

A *representative democracy* is one in which the general public does not directly control the government, but elects officials who they expect to act in their interest. Countries that function as representative democracies set clear, explicit limits on what elected officials can do. Traits that are consistent among all representative democracies include open elections, the forced acceptance of majority decisions, and a one person/one vote policy. In a representative democracy, power is given to the office, not to the holder of the office. Dissent and criticism of elected officials is not only tolerated in such as system, it is considered necessary to maintain effectiveness. The challenge of the representative democracy is to make sure that all groups in a society feel that they have a chance to express their views, and that minority groups are not trampled by the will of the majority.

## Mixed-Age or Multi-Age Grouping

Mixed-age or multi-age grouping refers to grouping children so that the age span of the class is greater than one year, as in the nongraded approach. Mixed-age and multi-age grouping emphasize teaching and curriculum practices that realize the greatest benefits from the cooperation and interaction of children of various ages. In multi-age classes, teachers encourage the children with different levels of development and experience to help each other with all classroom activities, including application and mastery of basic literacy and mathematical skills. But teachers should use small temporary subgroupings in mixed-age classes for groups of children who require the same types of instruction to help them acquire basic skills.

# Demography and Social Change

## State Theory and World System Theory of Modernization

The state theory of modernization supports the ideals of capitalism by maintaining that whenever the government is restricted from seizing private property, capitalism will develop and free markets will arise as people modernize and strive to become more productive. The world system theory of modernization, also known as the dependency theory, states that some nations modernize at the expense of less-developed nations, and that so long as this exploitation continues, the less-developed nations will be unable to improve their lot. This theory essentially takes the Marxist view of the capitalist society, in which those who own the means of production are able to maintain dominance over the workers, and applies it to the interactions of nations.

## Globalization

Globalization is the process whereby all the social groups in the world are being brought into closer connection with one another. This has occurred mainly through the advances in transportation and communication technology, although the era of colonialism also had the effect of shrinking the world. This phenomenon has in some cases made it more difficult for repressive regimes to isolate themselves; during the Tiananmen Square uprising in China, for instance, Western media was able to communicate with the student rebels and present their story to the rest of the world. Many observers lament globalization, however, because they feel it will homogenize culture and crowd out fascinating, but not economically successful, societies.

## Industrialization

*Industrialization* is the process through which manual labor gives way to technology as the source of production. The most dramatic era of industrialization was, of course, the Industrial Revolution of the mid-nineteenth century, which offers the best chance for sociologists to consider the effects of the process. Before industrialization, most societies were only able to manufacture enough to subsist on, and so they were quite vulnerable to natural disaster. Afterwards, however, the immense surplus of product, coupled with the fact that the means of production were held by a very small part of the population, led to great inequality in wealth. Marx blamed industrialization for alienating the worker from his product, and allowing him to be exploited by the bourgeoisie.

## Demography

*Demography* is the area of sociology that focuses on human populations, specifically how they grow, decline, or migrate. Demography often entails dividing up a population by gender, wealth, education, or some other variable, and then analyzing the variable's relation to life expectancy or fertility. Sociologists rely on censuses to supply most of the data for large-scale demography, though they often conduct their own statistical research when they are looking at smaller populations. In many impoverished countries, however, accurate data is difficult to obtain, both because of the obscurity of many people's homes and a long-standing association in the public mind of census-taking with taxation. Interestingly, demography was first used as a means of equitably distributing life insurance.

## Urbanization

*Urbanization* is the process whereby large groups of people leave behind rural village life and move to cities and their surrounding metropolitan areas. This phenomenon has been huge in the twentieth century. Some sociologists fear that this massive migration will obscure traditional values and norms, and that the pollution, crime, and anxieties of city life are the inevitable result.

Others suggest that the movement to cities might be a good thing for many societies, because it will bring diverse peoples into close contact with one another, and encourage the dialogue and cooperation that results in innovation. Frequently, urbanization has meant that social groups are based more on interest than on kinship.

## Census

A *census* is a population count, including data in categories like age, gender, occupation, marital status, etc. Although the first censuses, conducted by the Jews and Romans, were mainly for the purposes of taxation and conscription, modern societies use the census to plan the best use of resources. Most large societies conduct a regular census; in the United States, a census is conducted during the first year of every decade. There has often been controversy surrounding this practice, as in 1990, when the American government was sued for allegedly undercounting the poor. The *Domesday* (pronounced "doomsday") *Book* was the excellent census conducted by William the Conqueror after his conquest of England in 1066.

## Demographic Transition and the Demographic Transition Theory

A *demographic transition* is a shift in the trend of population, from high fertility coupled with high mortality to low fertility and mortality. Low mortality is quicker to arrive than low fertility, and so societies experiencing this transition often have ballooning populations for a period. The *demographic transition theory* suggests that demographic transition is the result of modernization, which has reduced the value and necessity of large families. At present, many of the Western economic powers, which have moved past their industrial period and into a quieter, post-industrial economy, have populations that are either stationary or shrinking. There is still some debate among sociologists as to whether this trend will also apply to other nations as they progress economically.

## Population Structures and Increases

An *expansive population structure* is an age structure in which each younger cohort is larger than the one before it, indicating population growth. In a society with a *stationary population structure*, younger birth cohorts are the same size as older ones, before the older are reduced by mortality. In such a society, population neither grows nor declines. A society with a *constrictive population structure* is one in which younger cohorts are smaller than the ones before them, indicating population decline. A population that exhibits *arithmetic increase* has a constant rate of growth or decline; in other words, the same number of units is added or subtracted during each cycle. If a population grows or declines at a rate that grows with each cycle, it is said to display *exponential increase*.

## Malthusian Theory of Population

The *Malthusian theory of population* (named after its originator, the British economist Thomas Malthus) asserts that populations will always reach, and rise somewhat above, the number that can be sustained, and then will be reduced by the positive checks on growth. *Positive checks*, according to Malthus, are the factors usually responsible for slowing or stopping population growth. They are war, famine, and disease. The cycle of growth and decline will repeat indefinitely. The Malthusian theory of population had an immediate effect on society; governments that had previously considered a large population (and hence large labor force) as a positive attribute soon became nervous about growth. After Malthus, the British support for a national census and for contraception skyrocketed.

## Carrying Capacity as Used in Sociology

The *carrying capacity* is the maximum number of people a given environment can sustain. Because humans are a species with a relatively low reproduction rate but a long life span, and are not really hunted by any other animals, they are required to regulate their own population to an extent. Of course, external factors like famine and disease will also diminish a population that has exceeded its carrying capacity. Some theorists have speculated that humanity's mastery of technology means that it can continually raise its carrying capacity, such that there is no real limit on population growth. This is countered by those who point out the limited number of natural resources; they say that while carrying capacity can be raised in the short term, the exploitation of resources will ultimately lead to catastrophe.

## Rates of Birth, Death, and Fertility

Sociologists use the rates of birth, death, and fertility to assess the economic effects on life in a particular society. A society's *crude death rate* is the total number of deaths for a year (or any other period) divided by the total population for that period. The *crude birth rate* of a society is its total number of births for a year (or other period) divided by the total population of that period. The *fertility rate* of a society is the total number of births in a year divided by the total number of women in their child-bearing years. In the United States, child-bearing years are considered to be between the ages of 15 and 44. A society's *age-specific death rate* is calculated as the number of deaths per year within a given age range divided by the total number of individuals within that age range.

## Sex Ratio and Infanticide

The *sex ratio* is calculated as the number of persons of one gender compared to the number of persons of the other gender. Usually, sociologists express this ratio as the number of males per hundred females. One of the major causes of imbalanced sex ratios is female infanticide. *Infanticide* is the practice of killing infants soon after birth. Often, the infant is simply left outside to die of exposure. Many societies have either promoted or tacitly condoned female infanticide, in the belief that males are better workers and of more service to the society. The result is typically a society in which females who survive are governed by oppressive norms, because, being fewer in number, they are in much higher demand and must prove loyalty through chastity and fidelity. Also, societies with many more males than females usually have higher rates of both prostitution and homosexuality.

## Growth Rates

*Growth rate* is the gain or loss of population, calculated by dividing the net gain or loss in a particular period by the population at the start of the period. The point at which the number of births equals the number of deaths is called the *replacement-level fertility*. It is also called the *zero population growth level*. The *infant mortality rate* is calculated as the annual number of deaths of children less than a year old. The *expectation of life* is the number of years an individual of a certain age can expect to live, given the present mortality rate in that society. The *gross reproduction rate* is the number of daughters a woman of a certain age is likely to produce, given the society's current fertility rates. The *net reproduction rate* is the number of daughters likely to live after being birthed by that woman.

## Compression of Morbidity and Its Relevance to Sociology

A *compression of morbidity* is a hypothetical situation in which life expectancy would increase, and people would lead relatively active and healthy lives. Hypothetically, this could happen in contemporary America if everyone stopped smoking and drinking, exercised regularly, drove the speed limit, or adopted any number of other safe habits. Sociologists are interested in the idea of the compression of morbidity because it illustrates the continual gulf between what societies should do and what they actually do. Sociologists suggest that a number of social factors contribute to a society's reluctance to take obviously positive measures: economic pressures, resistance to change, and self-destructiveness fueled by alienation and anxiety, just to name a few.

## Age Structure as Used in Sociology

A society's *age structure* is the various proportions of individuals of different ages. It is affected, of course, by the birth, death, and migration rates. Sociologists use age structure diagrams to help them discern how the society will grow in the future; for instance, a society that has grown rapidly may continue to grow even if the birth rate seems to level off to a replacement level. This is because, though each woman may be having fewer children, there are more women to have children. Government officials and planners also make much use of age structure figures, because they indicate what a society's needs will be in the future. In a society with a large infant population, for example, the school system must be prepared to handle more students in the coming years.

## Neighborhood Life-Cycle Model

The *neighborhood life-cycle model* is an approach used by sociologists to consider the transitions of neighborhoods through various stages. This model shows the process of neighborhood change as a series of invasion/succession events, creating a cycle of development, transition, downgrading, thinning out, and renewal. Neighborhoods can decline for a number of reasons. First of all, they may suffer from the gradual deterioration of infrastructure, as well as the accompanying aging of their human population. Also, their architecture may become outdated and unpopular. If they are centrally located within a city, they may suffer from the intrusion of a financial or industrial district. Sociologists note that not every neighborhood passes through these stages in a strict sense.

## Origins and the Major Features of the Multiple-Nuclei Model

The *multiple-nuclei model* is a way of looking at urban land use devised by Edward Ullman and Chauncy Harris. They suggested that cities developed as cluster of urban areas, each with its own nucleus or central point, and with its own specialized function. This model minimizes the importance of the central business district, which other urban models use as their starting-point. Instead, said Harris and Ullman, cities tend to group industries that have common needs together. A good example of this is a cluster of factories close to some body of water. The clustering of similar interests tends to perpetuate itself, moreover, as entrepreneurs take advantage of the similar tastes and needs of the people there; airports, for instance, tend to be slowly surrounded by hotels and restaurants.

## Origins and the Major Features of the Sector Model

Homer Hoyt developed the *sector model* to describe urban land use. In this model, cities develop a series of triangular, or pie-piece-shaped, sectors surrounding a central business district. This model was based on Hoyt's observation that low-income housing tended to be located close to railroad lines, and commercial districts near major roads. He predicted, then, that if a city had several transportation "spokes" emerging from a central business district, each "wedge" of this city would take on a different function: within residential wedges, for instance, lower-class housing would tend to be close to the turmoil of the central business district, while more expensive housing would crop up at the extremities of the city. This model anticipates the upper-class flight to the suburbs that has taken place in many communities.

## Origins and Major Features of the Concentric Zones Concept

The idea of *concentric zones* in city planning was developed by Ernest Burgess. He claimed that land would be in high demand as a city started up, and that the most efficient way to arrange the districts would be in concentric rings around a central business district. Around this business district would be a zone of light industrial activity. This area, according to Burgess, would be in transition and subject to high crime. After that would come several rings for residential use, with the lower class occupying the ring closest to the business district, and the status of the occupants rising as the zones edge outward. Chicago is a good example of a city that has developed in this fashion.

## Urban Ecology and Municipal Infrastructure

*Urban ecology* is the sociological approach to studying cities that focuses on the use of land, and how this use is determined by the interactions between various groups of people and their geographic environments. Sociologists who work in urban ecology are concerned with finding the best way to arrange groups of people so that urban environments remain livable and sustainable. To this end, they focus on the efficient flow of water and energy through the urban environment. This involves careful planning of the *municipal infrastructure*: the transportation, sewer, water, and police systems in a city. As the population of cities has risen dramatically over the past 150 years, sociologists have closely studied the effect of municipal infrastructure on social interaction.

## Gentrification

*Gentrification* is the conversion of working-class or poor neighborhoods into middle-class or upper-class neighborhoods. This has frequently occurred as members of the upper class who formerly would have escaped to the suburbs have opted instead for the convenience of inner-city neighborhoods. The inevitable result is a rise in property value and the displacement of the former residents who can no longer afford to live there. Some cities have gone to great lengths to prevent this from happening, sometimes even placing artificial restraints on rent adjustment. Many of the recent instances of gentrification have involved gay and lesbian people seeking to establish an enclave of like-minded people in an urban neighborhood.

## Political-Economy View as Used in Sociology

When sociologists commenting on urban trends refer to the *political-economy view*, they mean the view that the history of a city is simply the history of all the individuals and groups within it making decisions and acting in their own best interests. In other words, trends in urban growth have occurred because powerful interests made them so; these interests did not become powerful because of their skill in adapting to urban trends. The groups that are seen to dominate urban development are banks, corporations, real estate and construction industries, and local governments. As one would expect, the political-economy view asserts that their decisions are made to maximize profits and minimize expense.

## Peasants and Landless Laborers

*Peasants* are people who grow crops and livestock primarily for their own use, with their own labor and the help of simple technology. Peasants usually make up the bulk of the labor force in a pre-industrial, agrarian society. Because they are not incorporated, they are vulnerable to famine. However, they tend to work much less than those individuals who work for profit, because they are only concerned with making enough to survive. On the whole, peasants tend to be more politically and culturally conservative than city-dwellers. *Landless laborers* are any peasants or children of peasants who have lost ownership of the land that they cultivate. Individuals who were formerly hunters and gatherers and have become low-wage workers on somebody else's land may also be classified as landless laborers.

## Hunting and Gathering Societies

*Hunting and gathering societies* are considered the most primitive form of society. Such societies typically are composed of a small number of people who sustain themselves by wandering the land in search of edible plants and animals. Because of the importance of mobility in the hunting and gathering society, the social group is usually quite small. The average life span in these groups is short. Hunting and gathering societies typically have little in the way of hierarchy, since everyone must contribute to the quest for sustenance. In most cases, these kinds of societies gradually give way to agrarian societies, as people discover that they can increase their store of food by consciously encouraging the growth of certain plants and animals.

## Agrarian Societies

*Agrarian societies* are those that sustain themselves through farming. The successful maintenance of an agrarian society requires that about 95% of the population be involved in agriculture. Provided it is founded on arable land, an agrarian society can be independent and self-contained. Sociologists attribute the rise of the first cities to early agrarian societies, since they necessitate staying in one place for a long period. For this same reason, people in an agrarian society often live with their extended family. Recently, many critics of the post-industrial and informational societies have advocated a return to the agrarian model. They claim that the simplicity of life and emphasis on community in agrarian societies is a remedy for the supposed sterility and complexity of modern life.

## Industrial Society

*Industrial societies* are those in which the economy is based on manufacturing, which in large part is done by machines. The industrial society largely replaced the agrarian society in Western Europe and the United States in the nineteenth century, resulting in a number of cultural changes. For one thing, the industrial society typically becomes highly specialized, and creates a tremendous surplus of products. Inequalities in wealth and prestige are magnified, and the large underclass tends to reside in squalid conditions within a large city. In most industrial societies, organized religion loses some of its power, while the government bureaucracy expands its power. Overall, industrial societies display more reliance on science and rationalism, and less on traditional institutions like the family and church.

## Post-Industrial Society

In a *post-industrial society*, more of the economy is based on providing services than on manufacturing goods. In particular, post-industrial societies rely on banking and legal work to produce revenue. Since the citizens of such a society spend a larger amount of time interacting with one another than they do working with machines, sociologists have predicted there would be more emphasis on promoting social harmony and cooperation. Unfortunately, this idyllic version of the post-industrial society has not yet arisen; instead, societies that move beyond heavy manufacturing typically replace it with jobs in a very competitive labor market. Even new fields, such as computer technology, that were purported to bring better living conditions, have to this point only provided a new setting for the traditional clash between the classes.

## Metropolis and Megalopolis

A *metropolis* is a city and its sphere of influence. A city's *sphere of influence* is the area in which residents depend on it for jobs, media, recreation, and a sense of community. A *fixed-rail metropolis* is a city whose size and shape are determined by the routes of train and trolley systems. A *freeway metropolis* is one that developed after the advent of widespread automobile traffic, and therefore does not have a structure based on the rail system. Instead, it adjusts its network of roads in accordance with growth. A *megalopolis* is formed when two or more metropolises have grown so much that their borders touch one another.

### Urban Place and City

The United States census defines an *urban place* as a community that has at least 2500 citizens, the majority of whom do not farm. The census defines a *city* as a community that has at least 50,000 inhabitants. Sociologists have sharply disagreed about the effects of cities on human society. Some sociologists praise cities as places where social development can be accelerated, where innovation in science and the arts is spurred by the mingling of many different cultures. Other sociologists stress the negative aspects of cities: pollution, crime, anxiety. A great deal of debate has centered on the sense of community within a city: some sociologists, Tonnies included, suggest that the move from village life to urban life destroyed the continuity of human associations and alienated people from one another; other sociologists praise cities for providing a chance for communities based on common interest, rather than haphazard geographical arrangement.

### Suburb

A *suburb* is an urban place neighboring a city. It is typically dependent on the city for its economic livelihood. Suburbs are usually populated by the middle and upper classes. They offer several advantages to residents: lower real estate prices, and thus the chance to own a family home; the potential to form enclaves with those of a similar race or ethnicity; protection from the drug and crime problems of the inner city; and easy access to commercial districts. These communities have evolved over the past few decades from being "bedroom communities," in which all the residents commuted to the city for work every day, to being economic centers in their own right. This has resulted in massive population sprawl in the United States.

### Social Movements

A *social movement* is any organization created for the express purpose of causing or preventing a certain social change. Sociologists have speculated that there is more potential for social movements in contemporary society because the citizens are better educated and grouped more closely together, offering more chances for interaction. Social movements have distinct life cycles; they are created, gain strength, reach a climactic moment of either success or failure, and then fall apart. Although they are usually organized around a set of ideas, they are often catalyzed by the presence of a charismatic leader. Interestingly, the only enduring social movements are those that fail; successful movements, of course, have no need to continue.

### Collective Behavior and Resource Mobilization Approaches to Social Movements

The *collective behavior approach* to social movements suggests that social movements are eruptions of group activity symptomatic of some deep misgivings about the society. This approach emphasizes the importance of emotions and ideology in motivating group actions. The *resource mobilization approach* to social movements stresses the importance of human and material resources in the creation and success of social movements. This approach emphasizes the power of charismatic and influential leaders, as well as of rational planning. Of course, revolutions are never fully explicable by either of these approaches: the Russian Revolution, for instance, was motivated by the ideology of socialism, to be sure, but it was also successful because of the presence of charismatic leaders like Lenin and Trotsky.

## Rumors and Social Contagions in Sociological Terms

A *rumor*, in sociological terms, is any unverified story that circulates by word of mouth and is widely held to be true, despite universal ignorance of its source. *Social contagion* is the swift and unintentional spread of a mood or pattern of behavior from one individual to another. Usually, the spread of a social contagion can be traced to a particular event; in the case of the 1992 Los Angeles riots, this was the acquittal of the LAPD officers accused of beating Rodney King. People then gather together without any definite mood or set of norms to govern their behavior. Once a few individuals attract the attention of the others with some distinctive, extreme behavior, this mood becomes contagious in the group as a whole.

## Social Revolution

In sociology, a *social revolution* is defined as a rapid and far-reaching transformation of a society's social stratification system. It is different from a rebellion in that it produces structural change, and different from a revolutionary process like modernization in that it produces political change. The sociologist Theda Skocpol spent her career studying social revolutions, and pointed to three factors that distinguish them. For one, social revolutions are seldom begun intentionally; instead, they usually emerge from external causes like famines or war. Second, social revolutions are properly understood as reactions against the state, rather than against the ruling class. Finally, social revolutions are usually aided by either the help or the tacit approval of other nations.

## Countermovement and Counterrevolution

A *countermovement* is any social movement that arises in opposition to another social movement. Frequently, social movements aimed at changing social values or norms inspire conservative countermovements, aimed at preserving the status quo. A *counterrevolution*, then, is simply any organized resistance to a social revolution. Counterrevolutions may be conservative in nature, but they are also often led by members of the original revolution who have become disenchanted with its progress. For instance, many of Fidel Castro's opponents in Cuba have been those who supported the coup that overthrew Batista and put Castro in command. Sociologists have noted that the atmosphere of upheaval generated by revolutions makes them ripe for a series of counterrevolutions, which often have the effect of perverting the original revolutionary ideology.

## Revolution of Rising Expectations and the J-Curve Theory

A *revolution of rising expectations* occurs when the hope for change has exceeded actual change, thus maximizing social unrest and making it likely that people will take action to change their society. One might consider the American Revolution as a revolution of rising expectations, in that Americans were expecting a greater economic reward from the colonies' trade than they were receiving. The *J-curve theory* is based on the idea of the revolution of rising expectations. This theory asserts that societies will enter a period of intense crisis if living conditions suddenly worsen after a period of rapid improvement. A history of prosperity gives the people the expectation that it will continue indefinitely, and therefore any hardship is disappointing and maddening.

## Ecology and the Green Revolution

*Ecology* is the whole system of relationships between all organisms, including humans, plants, animals, and their environments. Sociologists are interested in ecology insofar as it is affected by social behavior. For instance, high populations can put a severe strain on the natural environment in which society dwells, to the point that the society may become unable to sustain itself. At present, the wealthy countries of the world are using more than their share of the natural resources of the earth, such that some sociologists are concerned about the implications for Western society.

This concern has in part been responsible for the Green Revolution, the development of new high-yield versions of cereal crops like wheat and corn.

# Praxis Practice Test

**1. The best definition of culture is:**

a. The actual expression of societal norms
b. The ideal of what should occur in a particular society
c. The universal practices evident in all societies
d. The sum of everything learned by participants in a society
e. The most common traits among all members of a society

**2. An accurate definition of society is:**

a. The most basic group in which humans and animals operate
b. A group which values working together above all else
c. A stated expectation of all members of a group
d. An expectation considered to be vital to a group's welfare
e. The usual manner of doing things according to tradition

**3. Which of the following best characterizes ethnocentrism?**

a. The conviction that one's personal culture is superior to others
b. The conviction that it is difficult to adapt to a new culture
c. The conviction that some cultures pre-date others
d. The conviction that matriarchal societies are superior
e. The conviction one's personal culture is inferior to others

**4. According to George Murdock, which of the following is not a general characteristic of all cultural practices?**

a. Religion
b. Folklore
c. Property disputes
d. Tool-making
e. Laws

**5. Which of the following values is not identifiable in American culture?**

a. A respect for education for all
b. A respect for philosophical thinking
c. A respect for progress
d. A respect for moderation in everything
e. A respect for humanitarianism

**6. All societies contain certain basic institutions. Which of the following is excluded from these basic institutions?**

a. Education
b. Government
c. Economic
d. Religious
e. Medical

**7. Stating that Americans begin families after marriage, when in fact they often have children outside the institution of marriage, is an example of:**

a. Stratification
b. Subculture
c. Counter-culture
d. Patterned evasion
e. Secularism

**8. The following statements are true of all societies with the exception of:**

a. Societies are where culture takes place
b. Societies are interdependent for the mutual survival of all
c. Members of a society live in a specific area
d. Sexual reproduction is the chief means of continuing a society
e. A primary method of organizing a society is according to labor tasks

**9. Which of the following does not exemplify a typical response to rapid change?**

a. Culture shock
b. Future shock
c. Cultural lag
d. Societal lag
e. Patterned evasion

**10. Many airports have not been improved so that they can accommodate advances in aviation. This is due to:**

a. Future shock
b. Cultural lag
c. Culture shock
d. Cultural configuration
e. Technological rush

**11. A sampling method used in survey research which relies upon established differences in populations is known as:**

a. Stratified sampling
b. Role sampling
c. Systematic sampling
d. Representative sampling
e. Correlational sampling

**12. All of the following processes represent stages of sociological research with the exception of:**

a. Identification of the problem to be studied
b. Selection and review of pertinent literature
c. Selection of the individual to be studied
d. Identification of research design
e. Formulating a hypothesis

**13. Which of these definitions best describes qualitative methods used in sociological research?**

a. Research methods which focus on measurement
b. Research methods which focus on statistics
c. Research methods which focus on quantification
d. Research methods which focus on studying change
e. Research methods which focus on personal observations

**14. Content analysis does not include the study of which of the following?**

a. Averages
b. Means
c. Percentages
d. Modes
e. Redundancy

**15. Which of the problems listed below does not provide an ethical dilemma for sociologists?**

a. Invasion of privacy of the group
b. Method of application of research
c. Possibility of harm to participants
d. Issues of individual consent
e. Full disclosure skewing research results

**16. Which of these theorists is credited with the founding of psychoanalysis?**

a. Sigmund Freud
b. George Herbert Mead
c. Charles Horton Cooley
d. Jean Piaget
e. Erving Goffman

**17. According to Jean Piaget, all of the following phases are a part of cognitive development with the exception of:**

a. The sensorimotor phase
b. The abstract operational phase
c. The preoperational phase
d. The concrete operational phase
e. The formal operational phase

**18. ___________ names a marriage in which one wife is simultaneously married to two or more husbands.**

a. Group marriage
b. Patrilocality
c. Polyandry
d. Nuclearity
e. Ritualism

**19. According to Max Weber, which group reflects the fundamental organization of all societies?**

a. A reference group
b. An in-group
c. A bureaucracy
d. A characteristic institution
e. Nuclear group

**20. Which of the following stages is not a recognized research stage?**

a. Identifying the problem to be studied
b. Finding the appropriate design for research
c. Screening the subjects
d. Explaining the final conclusion of the study
e. Selection and review of pertinent literature

**21. In a/an _____________society, the major focus is upon information, rather than upon material goods.**

a. Hunting and gathering
b. Post-industrial
c. Horticultural
d. Agricultural
e. Ideological

**22. If a man is concurrently described as being a psychologist, a husband, a father, and a respected member of the community, he is being defined according to his:**

a. Ascribed status
b. Master status
c. Achieved status
d. Status set
e. Salient status

**23. All of the descriptions listed below are characteristics of deviance with the exception of which one?**

a. It offers encouragement that societal controls work
b. It often correlates with high intelligence
c. It often correlates with mental illness
d. It often correlates with criminal behavior
e. It often correlates with great ambition

**24. The nursing profession is an example of which of the following sectors?**

a. The predominant sector
b. The economic sector
c. The social sector
d. The distributive sector
e. The tertiary sector

**25. Which of the following types of government has leaders who fail to recognize the limitations of their authority?**

a. Authoritarian
b. Totalitarian
c. Democratic
d. Systematic
e. Problematic

**26. According to Max Weber, what are the major categories of authority?**

I. Traditional authority
II. Rational-legal authority
III. Charismatic authority
IV. Democratic authority

a. I, II, and III only
b. I, III, and IV only
c. II, III, and IV only
d. I, II, and IV only
e. I, II, III, and IV

**27. Religion is not associated with which of the following societal functions?**

a. Theodicy
b. Theocracy
c. Codes of ethics
d. Personality
e. Historical condition

**28. Typical sources of stratification do not include:**

a. Race
b. Age
c. Gender
d. Sexual preference
e. Social status

**29. Which of the following characteristics are not exhibited by collective behavior?**

a. Fashion
b. Spontaneity
c. Stereotypes
d. Instability
e. Revolution

**30. According to C. Wright Mills, some examples of the power elite include all of the following with the exception of:**

a. Business executives
b. High-ranking military officers
c. Elected representatives
d. College professors
e. Appointed judges

**31. Which of the following are not qualities of participants in social groups?**

a. They tend to interrelate systematically
b. They tend to display similar qualities
c. They exhibit a mutual tendency towards awareness
d. They tend to join on a voluntary or involuntary basis
e. They tend to be interdependent

**32. The major features of a/an ___________society are the use of hand tools to cultivate plants and the domestication of animals:**

a. Horticultural and pastoral
b. Agricultural
c. Hunting and gathering
d. Industrial
e. Postindustrial

**33. Which of the following statements does not describe an agricultural society?**

a. This society is more technologically advanced than horticultural and pastoral societies.
b. Irrigation is an important tool for this society.
c. Draft animals are of considerable importance in this society.
d. It is impossible to have a big surplus in this society.
e. Permanent tools necessary for survival.

**34. All of the following descriptions are typical of an industrial society with the exception of:**

a. Machines are employed for production purposes
b. Energy sources are employed for production purposes
c. Autos were developed in this society
d. The principal focus of this society is gathering information
e. Radios were popularized by this society

**35. Sociocultural evolution:**

a. Describes the inclination of cultures to increase in complexity in the long run
b. Describes the interconnection which exists between people
c. Describes the quantity of cultural elements which are environmentally based
d. Describes a specific method of categorizing societies
e. Describes the change in language and art of a culture as it progresses

**36. Of the following statements, which one is not true of social mobility?**

a. It is sometimes relative
b. It is sometimes absolute
c. It can involve proceeding through various levels of social stratification
d. It is normally unrelated to structural mobility
e. It is relatively unhindered in an open stratification system

**37. Which of the characteristics mentioned below is not typical of social inequality?**

a. Different treatment because of sex
b. Different treatment because of health
c. Different treatment because of race
d. Different treatment because of age
e. Different treatment because of religion

**38. All of the following are recognized distinctions often leading to differential treatment in societies with the exception of:**

a. Gender differences
b. Age differences
c. Religious differences
d. Compatibility differences
e. Racial differences

**39. In general, sociologists have found that people from similar social strata share the following features except:**

a. They have similar opportunities in life
b. They benefit equally from societal advantages
c. They are affected similarly by societal disadvantages
d. They generally participate in social stratification
e. They generally attempt to be socially mobile

**40. Which of these sociologists subscribe to a functionalist view of social stratification?**

I. Max Weber
II. Karl Marx
III. Kingsley Davis
IV. Wilbert Moore
V. David Riesman

a. III and IV only
b. I and V only
c. II and V only
d. I and II only
e. I, II, III, and IV

**41. A grown daughter's living standards have improved beyond those of her mother. This is an example of:**

a. Social hierarchy
b. Absolute mobility
c. Relative mobility
d. Social stratification
e. Social mobility

**42. An inescapable consequence of social stratification is:**

a. Social mobility
b. Absolute mobility
c. Social hierarchy
d. Social injustice
e. Social inequality

**43. The sociologist who defines modern conflict theory according to educational credentials is:**

a. Karl Marx
b. Randall Collins
c. Ralf Dahrendorf
d. Max Weber
e. Kingsley Davis

**44. In the past century, the most conclusive theories regarding how unusual collective behavior is defined includes the:**

I. Contagion theory
II. Emergent-image theory
III. Confluence theory
IV. Convergence theory
V. Emergent-norm theory

a. I, IV, and V only
b. I, II, and III only
c. III, IV, and V only
d. I, II, and V only
e. II, IV, and V only

**45. The founders of the emergent-norm theory are:**

I. Gustave LeBon
II. Rodney King
III. Ralph Turner
IV. Karl Marx
V. Lewis Killian

a. III and V only
b. IV and V only
c. II and V only
d. I and II only
e. I, II, and III

**46. The father of the contagion theory is:**

a. Lewis Killian
b. Gustave LeBon
c. Ralph Turner
d. Karl Marx
e. Ralf Dahrendorf

**47. A teenager's high school friends pressure him to get drunk. If he succumbs to the pressure his behavior can be seen as an example of:**

a. Convergence theory
b. Emergent-norm theory
c. Survival of the fittest theory
d. Contagion theory
e. Exchange theory

**48. Convergence theory:**

a. Proposes that sociologists, like psychologists, are influenced by their own incentives
b. Proposes that a person is influenced more by his/her own incentives than by the group's incentives
c. Proposes that social stratification is influenced most by its own incentives
d. Proposes that economic change is influenced most by its own incentives
e. Proposes that the upper classes are influenced most by their own incentives

**49. An illustration of the emergent-norm theory in action is:**

a. An adult shoots a thief, and others fire their own shots shortly thereafter
b. A crowd storms through town to defend a wounded soldier
c. A father becomes threatened because his son is more successful than he is
d. A child attempts to convince a group that violence is wrong
e. A stadium audience starts booing a protester who stormed the field

**50. Which of the characteristics listed below is true of riots?**

a. They reflect a "keep-up-with-the-Joneses" mentality
b. They reflect a strong influence from peer envy
c. They take more time to complete than mob actions
d. They are more prone to violence than mob actions
e. Spread of social contagion is always based in fact

**51. Which of the problem(s) listed below would not pose an ethical problem for sociologists who are performing research?**

I. Concern about deceiving the individual
II. Concern about harm to the subjects studied
III. Concern about proper application of research results
IV. Concern about risks to the individual
V. Concern about participants' consent

a. II and III only
b. III and V only
c. I and IV only
d. I only
e. II, III, and V only

**52. According to Sigmund Freud, which statement is not true as regards personality?**

a. There are three key elements which shape personality
b. Consciousness is actually equated with the ego
c. The id provides a system of checks and balances for the ego
d. Identification is essential to personality development
e. Repression is crucial to personality development

**53. Which of the following statements do not reflect George Herbert Mead's beliefs about socialization?**

a. He believed that socialization leads to facility in identifying deviant behavior
b. He believed that socialization results in a predictive facility as regards human reactions
c. He believed that socialization results in adaptive abilities as regards human behavior
d. He believed that socialization results in facility in modeling human behavior
e. He believed that socialization involves a significant other and a generalized other

**54. According to Erving Goffman, which of the following statements is not true?**

a. The formation of the self is strongly correlated with feedback given by others
b. The formation of the self strongly reflects multiple human interactions
c. The formation of the self is strongly influenced by one's attempts to sway others
d. The differences between the authentic self and the public portrayal of self are known as role-distance
e. The dramaturgical approach involves controlling the way others perceive a person

**55. Charles Horton Cooley espoused all of the theories below with the exception of:**

a. The self-concept is established early in life
b. The self-concept is fragile and easily damaged
c. The self-concept undergoes constant reassessment
d. The self-concept is acquired through a "looking glass"
e. The self-concept is developed based on the treatment one receives from other members of society

**56. Which of the following phases are not included in Erik Erikson's phases of ego formation?**

a. The nurturing phase
b. The young adult phase
c. The change from home-to-school phase
d. The seasoned adult phase
e. The rebellious teenage phase

**57. Which of the following statements does not describe Lawrence Kohlberg's theories?**

a. He believed that moral reasoning evolves through six basic steps
b. He was strongly influenced by Jean Piaget
c. He was thought to be short-sighted in regards to women
d. He believed that adolescence was a key step in the development of morals
e. Moral reasoning is constant throughout one's life

**58. Which of the statements below does not describe Carol Gilligan's viewpoint?**

a. Women tend to deal with ethical challenges via a perspective of responsibility
b. Men tend to deal with ethical challenges via a perspective of ultimate results
c. Boys and girls present substantial differences as to how their psyches operate
d. The two sexes approach problem-solving differently because of their divergent societal roles
e. Pre-pubescent children's psyches operate similarly and diverge after puberty

**59. _______________ is the societal custom in which a husband simultaneously has two or more wives.**

a. Polygyny
b. Kinship
c. Group marriage
d. Patrilocality
e. Mormonism

**60. Which of the following statements is false in regards to deviance?**

a. A social group can frequently become united as a result of deviance
b. Clear boundaries of appropriate behavior are delineated by deviance
c. A reasonable method of protest is provided through deviance
d. Both formal and informal controls over society are provided by deviance
e. A significant result of deviance is that it often destroys a group

**61. ____________ is a simultaneous marriage between multiple women and multiple men.**

a. Monogamy
b. Group marriage
c. Mormonism
d. Mutual consent
e. Polygyny

**62. The fact that Americans forbid marriage between immediate family members is an example of:**

a. Monogamy
b. Polygamy
c. Exogamy
d. Kinship
e. Nuclearity

**63. If the authority of the family rests with the mother, this is an example of a:**

a. Matriarchy
b. Matrilocality
c. Matrilineal society
d. Matrimonial society
e. Matricentric society

**64. All of the following describe a patriarchy except:**

a. It is sometimes matrilineal
b. It is sometimes matrilocal
c. The levirate is sometimes present in this society
d. Primogeniture is sometimes present in this society
e. Father-rule is not necessary

**65. A __________ society is one in which the family's authority rests primarily with the father.**

a. Patrimonial
b. Patrilineal
c. Patronizing
d. Patriarchal
e. Paternal

**66. ____________ is the societal custom in which marriage is only permitted between individuals belonging to the same, or similar, groups.**

a. Endogamy
b. Nuclearity
c. Integration
d. Monogamy
e. Polyandry

**67. If a person marries once, later divorces, and then marries once again, this is an example of:**

a. Polygamy
b. Serial monogamy
c. Deviance
d. Matrimony
e. Stigma

**68. A father from a patriarchal society who passes on his property to his youngest son is practicing:**

a. Ultimogeniture
b. Primogeniture
c. Neolocality
d. Patrilocality
e. Parsimony

**69. A pattern of tracing family lineage through the mother's side of the family is an example of ___________ research.**

a. Matrilocal
b. Matriarchal
c. Matrilineal
d. Matrimonial
e. Maternal

**70. According to Edwin Sutherland, all of the following statements are true except:**

a. Primary groups are the breeding grounds for criminal behavior.
b. Social interaction is a means by which criminal behavior is learned.
c. Childhood is often the time of life in which people learn to be criminals.
d. Criminal behavior is tied to a belief in its advantages.
e. Criminal behavior is found more prevalently in people in the lower class.

**71. The teaching profession has recently evolved such that it now requires the presentation of technical material. However, this profession remains at a similar level socially. Thus, the teaching profession today is an example of:**

a. Relative stratification
b. Relative mobility
c. Relative orientation
d. Relative structure
e. Relative status

**72. Social stratification terminology includes all of the following except:**

a. False consciousness
b. Status attainment theory
c. Visibility
d. Caste system
e. Social bonds

**73. All of the following statements are interpretations of the bases of modern conflict theory with the exception of:**

a. It can be based upon conflicts between different groups.
b. It can be based upon ideological differences.
c. It can be based upon a struggle to acquire educational credentials.
d. It can be based upon an individual's struggles for self-awareness.
e. It can be based upon the struggle between individual desire and societal norms.

**74. Which of the following has a charismatic leader, voluntary membership, and reflects the most basic type of organizational structure possible?**

a. Church
b. Sect
c. Cult
d. Fad
e. Civil religion

**75. All of the characteristics presented below describe a church, with the exception of:**

a. It has a formal leader
b. Its membership is based upon social stratification
c. It is recognized as an institution
d. It is only possible to abandon membership involuntarily
e. It exists in a low state of tension with surrounding society

**76. Which of the following traits do not reflect faiths based in East Asia and parts of Southeast Asia?**

a. They emphasize the teaching and learning of religious doctrines.
b. They emphasize the value of self-understanding.
c. They value nature.
d. They revere multiple gods.
e. They did not originate with Abraham.

**77. Which of the following traits is not characteristic of collective behavior?**

a. It is inclined to be spontaneous
b. It is inclined to be devoid of any support from an institution
c. It is challenging to view it in action
d. It rarely changes
e. It is inclined to be unpredictable

**78. Which of the following statements most accurately defines propaganda?**

a. It describes an issue of public interest
b. It describes social stratification
c. It describes the opinions of the public
d. It entails efforts to alter public opinion
e. It is purely political

**79. Major studies of social problems resulting from social stratification worldwide include all of the following except:**

I. Domestic abuse
II. Clinical depression
III. Date rape
IV. Adolescent pregnancies

a. I, III, and IV only
b. II and IV only
c. IV only
d. I and III only
e. I, II, and III only

**80. Which of the dimensions mentioned below does not affect social stratification?**

I. Manual
II. Domestic
III. Environmental
IV. National
V. Ideological

a. II and V only
b. I, IV, and V only
c. I, II, III, and IV only
d. II only
e. V only

**81. Of the factors listed below, which are Max Weber's independent factors associated with his theory of social stratification?**

I. Social class
II. Personal power
III. Social status
IV. Race

a. I, III, and IV only
b. II and IV only
c. IV only
d. I and III only
e. I, II, and III only

**82. Max Weber believed that all of the following were fundamental classes of society with the exception of:**

a. The middle class
b. The most affluent class
c. The petite bourgeoisie
d. The class of manual laborers
e. White-collar workers

**83. A supervisor who needs to be firm with employees about output and deadlines but who also likes to go bowling with them on the weekends, can been seen as an example of:**

a. Role strain
b. Role conflict
c. Role play
d. Role reversal
e. Role distance

**84. Susan is a licensed psychologist. This description of Susan is her:**

a. Ascribed status
b. Inferred status
c. Achieved status
d. Master status
e. Adopted status

**85. According to Ferdinand Tonnies, a good definition of gemeinschaft is:**

a. Community
b. Society
c. Dyad
d. Triad
e. Role play

**86. Some major categories of groups which sociologists have traditionally studied include all with the exception of:**

a. Aggregates
b. Families
c. Peer groups
d. Conglomerates
e. Secondary groups

**87. If a sociologist were to write all potential research subjects' names on individual cards, shuffle them, and then choose a certain number of cards with names which would be appropriate for a study, she is putting together a _______________ sample.**

a. Representative
b. Random
c. Systematic
d. Stratified
e. Descriptive

**88. When Elton May found in his studies that the sociologist's presence during research can alter the behavior of the participants, he actually discovered the _________________.**

a. Control group effect
b. Content analysis effect
c. Random sample effect
d. Stratification effect
e. Hawthorne effect

**89. The sociologist who is credited with discovering the grand theory of society is:**

a. Talcott Parsons
b. Robert Merton
c. C. Wright Mills
d. Dennis Wong
e. Erving Goffman

**90. Which of the following is not representative of a group which is oriented towards religion?**

a. Cult
b. Sect
c. Church
d. Temple
e. Stratification

**91. Which of the activities listed below is not associated with the primary sector of the economy?**

a. Hunting deer
b. Gathering plants and herbs
c. Panning for gold
d. Farming
e. Manufacturing cars

**92. ____________ is an activity associated with the secondary sector of the economy.**

a. Panning for gold
b. Manufacturing weapons
c. Providing electrical wiring
d. Providing physical therapy
e. Teaching Spanish

**93. Robert works as an occupational therapist for the local public schools system. His profession is part of the ________ sector.**

a. Service
b. Manufacturing
c. Production
d. Cultivation
e. Free market

**94. ______________is a profession associated with the primary economic sector.**

a. Knitting
b. Making rugs
c. Mining diamonds
d. Mending clothes
e. Repairing jewelry

**95. The production and profitable sale of a variety of both goods and services includes which of the following economic sectors?**

I. Barter
II. Free market
III. Direct exchange
IV. Supply and demand
V. Service

a. I and IV only
b. II and III only
c. V only
d. I, III, and IV only
e. III and V only

**96. Economic distribution systems encompass all of the following with the exception of:**

a. The secondary sector
b. The free market system
c. The barter system
d. The direct exchange
e. The informal sector

**97. Which of the following is not true about racial socialization?**

a. Individuals within different racial groups are socialized differently.
b. Typically, it describes the experience of minorities within a society.
c. It may vary between racial or ethnic groups.
d. Only the most underprivileged races experience racial socialization.
e. It occurs when individuals interact with the society at large.

**98. Which one of the following statements is not descriptive of ethnicity?**

a. It sometimes refers to the ability of a group to move through the social strata
b. It sometimes refers to a group recognized by its shared language.
c. It sometimes refers to a population which shares a national heritage
d. It is sometimes used as a means of enacting social stratification
e. It is sometimes based on differences taught and learned in a particular culture

**99. Traits associated with gender differences include all of the following with the exception of:**

a. Hairstyles
b. Clothes
c. Family position
d. Professions
e. Ethnic roles

**100. Bill is a retired software engineer. At his previous job Bill earned $100,000 per year. Now that he has retired from that job, Bill is only offered a salary of $50,000 per year for the same type of work. This is an example of:**

a. Age conflict theory
b. Age stratification
c. Age exception
d. Age orientation
e. Age functionalism

# Answer Key and Explanations

**1. D:** Culture can best be defined as the sum of everything that is learned by participating in a society. Choice A is incorrect because it is the specific definition of real culture, rather than a general definition of culture itself. Choice B defines ideal culture; again, this is a specific definition of a type of culture, rather than a definition of culture itself. Choice C refers not to culture, but to a cultural universal. (E) is also incorrect because it is not a definition of culture.

**2. A:** A good definition of society is that it is the most basic group in which humans and animals operate. (B) and (C) are incorrect because they are not definitions of society. (D) is likewise wrong because it is the definition of a societal more. (E) is also incorrect because it describes a societal custom but is not.a definition of society itself.

**3. A:** A major characteristic of ethnocentrism is the conviction that one's personal culture is the superior one. (B) is incorrect because ethnocentrism does not include the belief that it is difficult to adapt to a new culture. (C) is wrong because ethnocentrism does not reflect a conviction that some cultures pre-date others. (D) is incorrect because ethnocentrism is not associated with the belief that matriarchal societies are superior. (E) is incorrect because the correct answer is (A).

**4. C:** According to George Murdock, it is the preponderance of property rights, rather than property disputes, which is a characteristic of all cultural practices. It may be that property disputes arise from the characteristic of property rights, but property disputes are not, in and of themselves, one of Murdock's cultural universals. (A) is incorrect because Mr. Murdock does describe religion as a characteristic of all cultural practices. (B) is wrong because folklore is also considered a cultural universal by Murdock. (D) and (E) are incorrect because both tool-making and laws are included in Murdock's definition of cultural universals and practices.

**5. B:** is correct because American culture does not respect philosophical thinking. (A) is incorrect because Americans do have a respect for education for all. (C) A respect for progress, (D) a respect for moderation in everything, and (E) a respect for humanitarianism are also all incorrect answers because they represent values which are easily identifiable within American culture.

**6. E:** Although medical institutions are found in many societies, they are not one of the basic institutions found in all societies. (A) Educational institutions, although they can vary widely in their levels of sophistication, are common to all societies. (B) Government is another type of basic institution since all societies must organize themselves or chaos ensues. (C) and (D), economic and religious institutions, are also types of basic institutions evident in all societies.

**7. D:** Patterned evasion can be defined as a large discrepancy between what people claim they do and what they actually do in practice. Although Americans do have children within the context of marriage, they also have many children outside of this institution. (A) Stratification and (E) secularism are concepts unrelated to patterned evasion, as are (B) subculture and (C) counter-culture.

**8. B:** Interdependence among societies for the purpose of mutual survival is not a characteristic of all societies. (A) All societies are considered to be locations in which culture takes place. (C) The statements that members of a society live in a specific area, and (D) that sexual reproduction is the chief means of continuing a society are both true of all societies. (E) The statement that a primary method of organizing a society is according to its labor tasks is also an accurate statement as regards all societies.

**9. D:** Societal lag is neither a recognized phenomenon of rapid social change, nor a typical reaction to it; the term is a meaningless one. (A) Culture shock, (B) Future shock, (C) Cultural lag, and (E) Patterned evasion are all examples of common reactions by members of a society to rapid social change.

**10. B:** The fact that numerous airports have not been upgraded to accommodate advances in aviation is an example of cultural lag. (A) Future shock, (C) culture shock, and (D) cultural configuration all describe other types of cultural phenomena which differ from cultural lag. (E) is not an actual phenomenon.

**11. A:** A sampling method in survey research which relies upon established differences in populations is an example of stratified sampling. (B) Role sampling and (E) correlational sampling are not recognized forms of sampling. (C) Systematic sampling and (D) representative sampling are also wrong answers because they refer to other types of sampling methods which differ from stratified sampling.

**12. C:** Selection of the individual to be studied is a stage in psychological research which focuses upon the individual, not a stage in sociological research which relies upon the study of a group. (A), (B), (D), and (E) are all recognized steps in sociological research.

**13. E:** Research methods which focus on personal observations are examples of qualitative methods employed in sociological research. (A), (B), and (C) are incorrect because they all refer to quantitative methods of sociological research. (D) is incorrect because research methods which rely upon studying change are not typical of qualitative methods of sociological research.

**14. E:** Redundancy is not a part of content analysis; it refers to a mathematical concept unrelated to this type of analysis. (A) Averages (B) means, (C) percentages, and (D) modes are all factors which are considered to be significant in content analysis.

**15. D:** Issues of individual consent do not provide an ethical dilemma for sociologists because their studies are focused upon groups, not upon individuals. Instead, these issues would provide an ethical dilemma for psychologists because their focus is upon individuals. (A) Invasion of the privacy of the group, (B) method of application of research, and (C) possibility of harm to participants, and (E) the possibility of full disclosure skewing research results are ethical dilemmas for sociologists.

**16. A:** Sigmund Freud is credited with the founding of psychoanalysis. (B) George Herbert Mead is incorrect because he was involved in social psychology, not psychoanalysis. (C) Charles Horton Cooley is also an incorrect answer because he was a theorist with a background in economics and social psychology. (D) Jean Piaget and (E) Erving Goffman are also incorrect choices because they were, respectively, theorists involved in psychology and sociology.

**17. B:** The abstract operational phase is not one of Jean Piaget's phases of cognitive development. (A) The sensorimotor phase, (C) the preoperational phase, (D) the concrete operational phase, and (E) the formal operational phase are all, according to Jean Piaget, phases of cognitive development.

**18. C:** Polyandry is the type of marriage in which one wife is simultaneously married to two or more husbands. (A) Group marriage is incorrect because it describes an arrangement in which several wives are simultaneously married to several husbands. (B) Patrilocality, (D) nuclearity and (E) ritualism are also incorrect choices because they represent concepts unrelated to polyandry.

**19. D:** According to Max Weber, a characteristic institution reflects the fundamental organization of all societies. (A) A reference group and (B) an in-group are not the right answers because they refer to other phenomena unrelated to a characteristic institution. (C) A bureaucracy is a wrong choice because it reflects the basic organization of some societies, but not of all societies. (E) Nuclear group is not a sociological term; not all societies are organized by nuclear family.

**20. C:** Screening the subjects is not recognized as a stage of research. (A) Identifying the problem to be studied, (B) finding the appropriate design for research, (D) explaining the final conclusion of the study, and (E) selection and review of pertinent literature are recognized stages of research.

**21. B:** A post-industrial society's major focus is upon information, rather than upon material goods. (A) A hunting and gathering society, (C) a horticultural society, (D) an agricultural society and (E) an ideological society all have different focuses other than information.

**22. D:** A status set accurately defines multiple roles of the man described. (A) Ascribed status, (B) master status, (C) achieved status, and (D) salient status all describe single (rather than multiple) roles which a man might assume.

**23. B:** Deviance does not normally correlate with high intelligence. (A) It offers encouragement that societal controls work, (C) it often correlates with mental illness, (D) it often correlates with criminal behavior, and (E) it often correlates with great ambition are all incorrect choices because they all represent characteristics of deviance.

**24. E:** The nursing profession is an example of the tertiary sector. (A) The predominant sector, (B) the economic sector, (C) the social sector, and (D) the distributive sector are all incorrect answers because they are not associated with the nursing profession.

**25. B:** The leaders of a totalitarian government fail to recognize the boundaries of their authority. (A) and (C) are incorrect because there are discernible boundaries as regards the authority of both authoritarian and democratic governments. (D) Systematic and (E) problematic governments are not recognized types of government.

**26. A:** According to Max Weber, traditional authority (I), rational-legal authority (II), and charismatic authority (III) are the major categories of authority. Democratic authority (IV) is not a category of authority recognized by Weber. (B), (C), (D), and (E) are wrong because they all contain the incorrect answer, democratic authority (IV).

**27. B:** Theocracy is not a societal function normally associated with religion. It refers, instead, to a type of government. (A), theodicy, (C) codes of ethics, (D) personality, and (E) historical condition are all incorrect because they are societal functions which are usually associated with religion.

**28. E:** Social status is not a typical source of stratification. (A) Race, (B) age, (C) gender, and (D) sexual preference are all incorrect answers because they do represent typical sources of societal stratification.

**29. C:** Stereotypes are not among the characteristics usually associated with collective behavior. (A) Fashion, (B) spontaneity, (D) instability, and (E) revolution are all incorrect answers because they represent characteristics normally associated with collective behavior.

**30. D:** According to C. Wright Mills, the power elite does not include the category of college professors. (A) Business executives, (B) high-ranking military officers, and (C) and (E) government leaders are all incorrect answers because they are all components of C. Wright Mill's power elite.

**31. B:** Participants in social groups do not tend to display similar qualities. This description refers, instead, to a social category. (A), (C), (D), and (E) are all incorrect answers because they all accurately represent qualities of participants in social groups.

**32. A:** The major features of a horticultural and pastoral society are the use of hand tools to cultivate plants and the domestication of animals. (B) Agricultural, (C) hunting and gathering, (D) industrial, and (E) postindustrial are all incorrect answers because these societies do not display the major features of cultivating plants and the domestication of animals.

**33. D:** It is possible to produce big surpluses in an agricultural society. (A), (B), (C), and (D) are all incorrect answers because they all accurately represent characteristics typically found in an agricultural society.

**34. D:** The type of society whose primary focus is to gather information is an information society, not an industrial one. (A), (B), (C), and (E) are all incorrect answers because they are all characteristics of an industrial society.

**35. A:** The best characterization of sociocultural evolution is that it describes the inclination of organizations to increase in complexity in the long run. Choice B is incorrect because it is the description of society, not of sociocultural evolution. Choice C and Choice D are also wrong because they describe the ecological approach, not sociocultural evolution. (E) is incorrect because it does not refer to the increasing complexity of cultures.

**36. D:** The statement that social mobility is unrelated to structural mobility is incorrect. In fact, the opposite is true: social mobility is related to structural mobility. (A), (B), (C), and (D) are incorrect because they do describe characteristics of social mobility.

**37. B:** Different treatment due to health issues is a concept unrelated to social inequality. (A) Different treatment because of sex, (C) different treatment because of race, (D) different treatment because of age, and (E) different treatment because of religion are all incorrect choices because they are characteristics typical of social inequality.

**38. D:** is correct because compatibility differences are not among the recognized distinctions often leading to differential treatment in societies. (A) Gender differences, (B) age differences, (C) religious differences, and (E) racial differences are all incorrect answers because they all represent recognized societal distinctions which often lead to differential treatment.

**39. E:** Although some people from the same social stratum may attempt to be socially mobile, it is incorrect to assume that there is a general tendency among all to aspire towards social mobility. (A), (B), (C), and (D) are incorrect because they each represent characteristics of people from the same social stratum.

**40. A:** Kingsley Davis (III) and Wilbert Moore (IV) both subscribe to a functionalist view of social stratification. (B), (C), (D), and (E) are incorrect because they include sociologists who do not subscribe to a functionalist view of social stratification (Weber, Marx, and Riesman).

**41. B:** A grown daughter's living standards improving beyond those of her mother represents absolute mobility. (A) Social hierarchy, (C) relative mobility, (D) social stratification, and (E) social mobility are incorrect selections because they are not examples of this generational improvement in living standards.

**42. C:** Social hierarchy is an inescapable consequence of social stratification. (A) Social mobility, (B) absolute mobility, (D) social injustice, and (E) social inequality are all incorrect answers because they are not inescapable consequences of social stratification.

**43. B:** Randall Collins is the sociologist who defines modern conflict theory according to educational credentials. (A) Karl Marx, (C) Ralf Dahrendorf, (D) Max Weber, and (E) Kingsley Davis do not subscribe to this theory.

**44. A:** During the past 100 years, the most conclusive theories as regards defining unusual collective behavior include the: (I) contagion theory, (IV) convergence theory, and (V) emergent-norm theory. (II) Emergent-image theory and (III) confluence theory are not recognized theories for defining unconventional behavior.

**45. A:** is the correct answer because it refers to (III), Ralph Turner, and (V), Lewis Killian, who together developed the emergent-norm theory. (B), (C), and (D) are all wrong because none of them include the names of these two founders of the theory. (E) is incorrect because it includes LeBon and King and not Killian.

**46. B:** is correct because Gustave LeBon is the father of the contagion theory. (A) Lewis Killian, (C) Ralph Turner, (D) Karl Marx, and (E) Ralf Dahrendorf are incorrect answers because they had no involvement in developing this theory.

**47. D:** If a teenager gives in to the pressures of his high school friends, his behavior is an example of contagion theory. (A) Convergence theory and (B) emergent-norm theory are wrong because they are unrelated to this example. (E) Exchange theory is incorrect because it describes the ways people benefit from each other in social interaction.

**48. B:** The best definition of convergence theory is that a person is influenced more by his/her own incentives than by those of the group. (A), (C), (D), and (E) are all incorrect because none of them offer definitions of the convergence theory.

**49. A:** If an adult shoots a thief and others fire their own shots shortly thereafter, this is an illustration of the emergent-norm theory in action. (B), (C), and (D) are incorrect because they are not demonstrations of this theory. (E) is wrong because protesting is not morally ambiguous and booing is not a new norm.

**50. C:** Riots take more time to complete than mob actions. (A), (B), and (D) are all wrong choices because they are not true statements about riots. (E) Spread of social contagion, which can lead to riots, does not have to be based in fact or verified.

**51. C:** contains the correct answers: (I) concern about deceiving the individual, and (IV) concern about the risks to the individual. Furthermore, (I) and (IV) are both concerned with the individual; this is actually the focus of psychology rather than of sociology. II, III, and V all pose ethical problems for the sociologist since they are focused upon the group, which is the basis for sociological study.

**52. C:** The statement that the id provides a system of checks and balances for the ego is not true of Freud's theories in regards to personality. In fact, the opposite is true. Freud believed that the ego provides a system of checks and balances for the id. (A), (B), (D), and (E) are all incorrect answers because each of them represent true statements made by Freud.

**53. A:** George Herbert Mead did not believe that socialization leads to a facility in identifying deviant behavior. (B), (C), (D), and (E) all accurately refer to Mead's theories.

**54. E:** The dramaturgical approach involves "impression management", which hopes to influence how a person is perceived by others. Controlling the way others perceive a person is not possible. (A), (B), and (C) represent different facets of Goffman's beliefs about the self. (D), which describes the differences between the authentic self and the public portrayal of self, is Goffman's definition of role-distance.

**55. B:** Charles Horton Cooley did not espouse the theory that the self-concept is fragile and easily damaged. (A), (C), (D), and (E) are all among Cooley's theories.

**56. E:** is the correct answer because the rebellious teenage phase is not one of Erikson's phases of ego formation. (A), (B), (C), and (D) are all incorrect answers in that they each accurately represent a particular phase of ego formation as described by Erikson.

**57. E:** Kohlberg theorized that moral thinking developed as people grew older, not that it was constant throughout life. (A) Kohlberg believed that moral reasoning evolves through six basic steps, (B) he was strongly influenced by Jean Piaget, (C) many have considered him to have been short-sighted in regard to women, and (D) he believed that adolescence was a key step in the development of morals.

**58. E:** According to Carol Gilligan, (A) women tend to approach ethical challenges from the perspective of responsibility, (B) men tend to approach ethical challenges from the perspective of ultimate results, (C) boys and girls present fundamental differences as to how their psyches operate, and (D) the two sexes approach problem-solving differently because of their divergent social roles. (E) is not part of Carol Gilligan's viewpoint.

**59. A:** Polygyny is the societal custom in which a husband simultaneously has two or more wives. (B) Kinship, (C) group marriage, and (D) patrilocality do not describe this type of societal custom. (E) Mormonism is incorrect because it describes a specific religion, not a type of societal custom.

**60. E:** A significant result of deviance is not that it often destroys a group. (A), A social group can frequently become united as a result of deviance, (B), clear boundaries of appropriate behavior are delineated by deviance, (C), a reasonable method of protest is provided through deviance, and (D), both formal and informal controls over society are provided by deviance, are all incorrect answers because they are true of deviance.

**61. B:** Group marriage is a type of marriage in which multiple women are simultaneously married to multiple men. (A) Monogamy is incorrect because it defines a marriage between one man and one woman only. (C) Mormonism is wrong because it describes a religion, not a type of marriage. (D) Mutual consent is an incorrect answer because it is not a recognized form of marriage. (E) Polygyny, which refers to the societal custom in which the husband simultaneously has two or more wives, is also wrong because it refers to a different type of marriage.

**62. C:** The fact that Americans forbid marriage between immediate family members is an example of exogamy. (A) Monogamy and (B) polygamy are incorrect because they refer to certain types of marriage which differ from exogamy. (D) Kinship and (E) nuclearity are wrong answers because they are concepts which are not associated with exogamy.

**63. A:** If the authority of the family rests with the mother, this is an example of a matriarchy. (B) Matrilocality is incorrect because it describes the custom of newlyweds living under the same roof as the wife's extended family. (C) Matrilineal society is wrong because it refers to the procedure of tracing a family's lineage through the mother. (D) Matrimonial society is incorrect because it is not a recognized type of society. (E) Matricentricity does not describe patterns of authority.

**64. E:** Patriarchy describes a system in which family systems are organized around father-rule and male authority. (A), which states that a patriarchy can be matrilineal, and (B), which states that a patriarchy can be matrilocal, are both incorrect answers because they are, in fact, characteristics of patriarchies. (C), which states that the levirate is sometimes present in this society, and (D), which states that primogeniture is sometimes present in this society, are also incorrect choices because they are possible traits of a patriarchy as well.

**65. D:** A patriarchal society is one in which the family's authority rests with the father. (A) Patrimonial is incorrect because it describes a different type of society which is based upon its ancestors. (B) Patrilineal is a wrong choice because it refers to a method of tracing family lineage, not to a type of society. (C) Patronizing is incorrect because it is not a recognized type of society. (E) Paternal is an incorrect answer because it refers to anything associated with fatherhood, and because it is also not a recognized type of society.

**66. A:** Endogamy is the societal custom of only allowing marriage between individuals belonging to the same, or similar, groups. (B) Nuclearity is wrong because it is not a recognized societal custom. (C) Integration is an incorrect answer because it represents a social concept different from endogamy. (D) Monogamy and (E) polyandry are both wrong because they refer to marital arrangements which differ from endogamy.

**67. B:** Serial monogamy describes a situation in which a person marries once, later divorces, and then marries once again. (A) Polygamy is incorrect because it describes the societal custom of having more than one spouse at a time. (C) Deviance is a social concept unrelated to serial monogamy and is, therefore, a wrong answer. (D) Matrimony is incorrect because it is merely another word for marriage. (E) is incorrect because stigma is not associated with serial monogamy.

**68. A:** If a father from a patriarchal society passes on his property to his youngest son, he is practicing ultimogeniture. (B) Primogeniture is incorrect because it refers to the practice of a father's passing his property to his eldest son, not his youngest. (C) Neolocality and (D) patrilocality are incorrect because they represent concepts unrelated to ultimogeniture. (E) Parsimony is incorrect because is it not a societal practice; it is merely another word for stinginess.

**69. C:** A pattern of tracing family lineage through the mother's side of the family is an example of matrilineal research. (A) Matrilocal is incorrect because it describes the custom in which newlyweds live under the same roof with the wife's extended family. (B) Matriarchal is wrong because it refers to a society in which the mother holds the authority. (D) Matrimonial is incorrect because it refers to anything associated with marriage, not specifically to the practice of tracing family lineage. (E) Maternal is also not the correct answer because it is a general term used to describe anything about mothers and is not a type of family research.

**70. E:** Sutherland studied white-collar crime in contrast to his predecessors who thought that criminal behavior was found more prevalently in people in the lower class. According to Southerland, (A) primary groups are the breeding ground for criminal behavior, (B) social interaction can teach criminal behavior, (C) childhood is often the time when people learn to be criminals, and (D) criminal behavior is tied to a belief in its advantages are all beliefs which are fundamental to Sutherland's theories of criminal behavior.

**71. B:** The teaching profession today is an example of relative mobility. (A) Relative stratification, (C) relative orientation, (D) relative structure, and (E) relative status are all incorrect because they are not recognized patterns of social stratification.

**72. E:** Social bonds is the only phrase that does not pertain to social stratification, or social layering in accordance with power, wealth, or honor. This can happen according to race and ethnicity, gender, age, and sexual preference, among other things. Marx's false consciousness, status attainment theory, visibility and markers, and India's caste system are all related to social stratification.

**73. D:** Modern conflict theory does not place an emphasis upon an individual's self-awareness. (A), (B), (C), and (E) each accurately describe interpretations of the bases of modern conflict theory.

**74. C:** A cult is a group which has a charismatic leader, voluntary membership, and reflects the most basic type of organizational structure possible. (A), Church, and (B), sect, may or may not have charismatic leaders, voluntary membership and the most basic type of organizational structure, making these choices incorrect. (D) Fad is incorrect because it doesn't have a leader or membership and (E) is wrong because, among other things, it is not the most basic type of organizational structure.

**75. B:** A church's membership is not based upon social stratification. (A), (C), (D), and (E) all describe traits regularly associated with the definition of a church.

**76. A:** Faiths based in East Asia and parts of Southeast Asia do not emphasize the teaching and learning of religious doctrines. (B), (C), (D), and (E) do, in fact, represent traits present in the faiths of Southeast Asia and East Asia.

**77. D:** The statement that collective behavior rarely changes is false. In fact, the opposite is true; it changes a great deal. (A), (B), (C), and (E) are all incorrect answers because they are all characteristics of collective behavior.

**78. D:** is the correct answer because the most accurate definition of propaganda is that it entails efforts to alter public opinion. (A), (B), and (C) are incorrect answers because they are not definitions of propaganda. (E) is wrong because propaganda is not just political.

**79. D:** I and III only is the correct answer because there are no major studies of social problems resulting from social stratification worldwide in the areas of (I) domestic abuse or (III) date rape.

**80. C:** Social stratification is not affected by (I) manual, (II) domestic, (III) environmental, and/or (IV) national dimensions. A, B, and E are all incorrect because they all contain the wrong answer, (V). (D) is wrong because it fails to mention the additional correct answers (I), (III), and (IV).

**81. E:** Race (IV) is not one of Max Weber's independent factors which form the basis for his theory of stratification. (I), (II), and (III) are all incorrect because they are among Weber's independent factors forming his theory of stratification.

**82. A:** The middle class is not one of Max Weber's major classes of society. (B) The most affluent class (upper class), (C) the petite bourgeoisie, (D) the class of manual laborers, and (E) white-collar workers are Max Weber's major societal classes.

**83. A:** If a supervisor who needs to be firm with employees as regards output and deadlines also likes to go bowling with them on the weekends, this is an example of role strain. (B) Role conflict,

(C) role play, (D) role reversal, and (E) role distance are all incorrect answers because they do not describe the given situation.

**84. C:** The description of Susan as a licensed psychologist, a status which she has personally attained, is a description of her achieved status. (A) Ascribed status is incorrect because it refers to a different type of status which is assigned to an individual and has nothing to do with one's own personal achievements. (B) Inferred status and (E) adopted status are not recognized types of status. (D) Master status is incorrect because it represents a more comprehensive definition of someone's status than does achieved status.

**85. A:** According to Ferdinand Tonnies, a good definition of gemeinschaft is community. (B) Society, (C) dyad, (D) triad, and (E) role play are all wrong because they are not definitions of gemeinschaft.

**86. D:** Conglomerates is the correct answer because this is not a major category of groups which sociologists have traditionally studied. (A) Aggregates, (B) families, (C) peer groups, and (E) secondary groups are all incorrect answers because they all represent important categories of groups which sociologists have traditionally studied.

**87. B:** If a sociologist were to blindly choose the necessary number of cards with names on them for potential research subjects, she is putting together a random sample. (A) Representative sample, (C) systematic sample, and (D) stratified sample are incorrect answers because they represent different types of samples than do random samples. (E) Descriptive sample is wrong because it is not a recognized type of sample.

**88. E:** When Elton May found in his studies that the sociologist's presence during research can alter the behavior of the participants, he actually discovered the Hawthorne effect. (A) Control group effect, (B) content analysis effect, (C) random sample effect, and (D) stratification effect are not recognized influences upon the research subject's behavior.

**89. A:** Talcott Parsons is the sociologist credited with discovering the grand theory of society. (B) Robert Merton, (C) C. Wright Mills, (D) Dennis Wong, and (E) Erving Goffman are all incorrect answers because they are not founders of this theory.

**90. E:** Stratification is the correct answer because it is not a type of religious group. (A) Cult, (B) sect, (C) church, and (D) temple are all incorrect answers because they all represent various types of religious groups.

**91. E:** Manufacturing cars is the correct answer because it is not associated with the primary sector of the economy. It is, instead, associated with its secondary sector. (A) Hunting deer, (B) gathering plants and herbs, (C) panning for gold, and (D) farming are all incorrect answers because they are all associated with the primary economic sector.

**92. B:** Manufacturing weapons is the correct answer because it is associated with the secondary sector of the economy. (A) Panning for gold is incorrect because it is an activity associated with the primary economic sector, not with the secondary one. (C) Providing electrical wiring, (D) providing physical therapy, and (E) teaching Spanish are all wrong answers because they are associated with the tertiary economic sector, not the secondary one.

**93. A:** As an occupational therapist, Robert works in the service sector. (B) Manufacturing is incorrect because it is a profession associated with the secondary economic sector. (C) Production, (D) cultivation, and (E) free market are all wrong answers because they are not recognized economic sectors.

**94. C:** Mining diamonds is a profession associated with the primary economic sector. (A) Knitting, (D) mending clothes, and (E) repairing jewelry are all incorrect answers because they are professions associated with the tertiary sector, not with the primary economic sector. (B) Making rugs is also a wrong answer because it is a profession associated with the secondary economic sector.

**95. C:** The production and profitable sale of a variety of both goods and services includes the service sector (V) only. (A), (B), (D), and (E) are all incorrect answers because they each include one or more incorrect choices.

**96. A:** Economic distribution systems encompass all of the systems mentioned except the secondary sector. (B) The free market system, (C) the barter system, (D) the direct exchange, which is another way of describing the barter system, and (E) the informal sector each represent a type of economic distribution system.

**97. D:** Every individual in a multi-racial society undergoes a degree of racial or ethnic socialization. The statements in (A), (B), (C), and (E) all describe racial socialization.

**98. A:** The statement that ethnicity sometimes refers to the ability of a group to move through the social strata is incorrect. This definition is actually of social mobility, not of ethnicity. (B) It sometimes refers to a group recognized by its shared language, (C) it sometimes refers to a group which shares a national heritage, (D) it is sometimes used as a means of enacting social stratification, and (E) it is sometimes based upon differences taught and learned in the particular culture are all incorrect answers because they are descriptive of ethnicity.

**99. E:** Traits associated with gender differences include all but differences in ethnic roles. (A) Differences in hairstyles, (B) differences in clothing, (C) differences in family position, and (D) differences in professions are all incorrect answers because they all represent traits associated with gender differences.

**100. B:** This treatment of Bill is an example of age stratification. (A) Age conflict theory, (C) age exception, (D) age orientation, and (E) age functionalism are not recognized theories in sociology.

# How to Overcome Test Anxiety

Just the thought of taking a test is enough to make most people a little nervous. A test is an important event that can have a long-term impact on your future, so it's important to take it seriously and it's natural to feel anxious about performing well. But just because anxiety is normal, that doesn't mean that it's helpful in test taking, or that you should simply accept it as part of your life. Anxiety can have a variety of effects. These effects can be mild, like making you feel slightly nervous, or severe, like blocking your ability to focus or remember even a simple detail.

If you experience test anxiety—whether severe or mild—it's important to know how to beat it. To discover this, first you need to understand what causes test anxiety.

## Causes of Test Anxiety

While we often think of anxiety as an uncontrollable emotional state, it can actually be caused by simple, practical things. One of the most common causes of test anxiety is that a person does not feel adequately prepared for their test. This feeling can be the result of many different issues such as poor study habits or lack of organization, but the most common culprit is time management. Starting to study too late, failing to organize your study time to cover all of the material, or being distracted while you study will mean that you're not well prepared for the test. This may lead to cramming the night before, which will cause you to be physically and mentally exhausted for the test. Poor time management also contributes to feelings of stress, fear, and hopelessness as you realize you are not well prepared but don't know what to do about it.

Other times, test anxiety is not related to your preparation for the test but comes from unresolved fear. This may be a past failure on a test, or poor performance on tests in general. It may come from comparing yourself to others who seem to be performing better or from the stress of living up to expectations. Anxiety may be driven by fears of the future—how failure on this test would affect your educational and career goals. These fears are often completely irrational, but they can still negatively impact your test performance.

## Elements of Test Anxiety

As mentioned earlier, test anxiety is considered to be an emotional state, but it has physical and mental components as well. Sometimes you may not even realize that you are suffering from test anxiety until you notice the physical symptoms. These can include trembling hands, rapid heartbeat, sweating, nausea, and tense muscles. Extreme anxiety may lead to fainting or vomiting. Obviously, any of these symptoms can have a negative impact on testing. It is important to recognize them as soon as they begin to occur so that you can address the problem before it damages your performance.

The mental components of test anxiety include trouble focusing and inability to remember learned information. During a test, your mind is on high alert, which can help you recall information and stay focused for an extended period of time. However, anxiety interferes with your mind's natural processes, causing you to blank out, even on the questions you know well. The strain of testing during anxiety makes it difficult to stay focused, especially on a test that may take several hours. Extreme anxiety can take a huge mental toll, making it difficult not only to recall test information but even to understand the test questions or pull your thoughts together.

## Effects of Test Anxiety

Test anxiety is like a disease—if left untreated, it will get progressively worse. Anxiety leads to poor performance, and this reinforces the feelings of fear and failure, which in turn lead to poor performances on subsequent tests. It can grow from a mild nervousness to a crippling condition. If allowed to progress, test anxiety can have a big impact on your schooling, and consequently on your future.

Test anxiety can spread to other parts of your life. Anxiety on tests can become anxiety in any stressful situation, and blanking on a test can turn into panicking in a job situation. But fortunately, you don't have to let anxiety rule your testing and determine your grades. There are a number of relatively simple steps you can take to move past anxiety and function normally on a test and in the rest of life.

## Physical Steps for Beating Test Anxiety

While test anxiety is a serious problem, the good news is that it can be overcome. It doesn't have to control your ability to think and remember information. While it may take time, you can begin taking steps today to beat anxiety.

Just as your first hint that you may be struggling with anxiety comes from the physical symptoms, the first step to treating it is also physical. Rest is crucial for having a clear, strong mind. If you are tired, it is much easier to give in to anxiety. But if you establish good sleep habits, your body and mind will be ready to perform optimally, without the strain of exhaustion. Additionally, sleeping well helps you to retain information better, so you're more likely to recall the answers when you see the test questions.

Getting good sleep means more than going to bed on time. It's important to allow your brain time to relax. Take study breaks from time to time so it doesn't get overworked, and don't study right before bed. Take time to rest your mind before trying to rest your body, or you may find it difficult to fall asleep.

Along with sleep, other aspects of physical health are important in preparing for a test. Good nutrition is vital for good brain function. Sugary foods and drinks may give a burst of energy but this burst is followed by a crash, both physically and emotionally. Instead, fuel your body with protein and vitamin-rich foods.

Also, drink plenty of water. Dehydration can lead to headaches and exhaustion, especially if your brain is already under stress from the rigors of the test. Particularly if your test is a long one, drink water during the breaks. And if possible, take an energy-boosting snack to eat between sections.

Along with sleep and diet, a third important part of physical health is exercise. Maintaining a steady workout schedule is helpful, but even taking 5-minute study breaks to walk can help get your blood pumping faster and clear your head. Exercise also releases endorphins, which contribute to a positive feeling and can help combat test anxiety.

When you nurture your physical health, you are also contributing to your mental health. If your body is healthy, your mind is much more likely to be healthy as well. So take time to rest, nourish your body with healthy food and water, and get moving as much as possible. Taking these physical steps will make you stronger and more able to take the mental steps necessary to overcome test anxiety.

## Mental Steps for Beating Test Anxiety

Working on the mental side of test anxiety can be more challenging, but as with the physical side, there are clear steps you can take to overcome it. As mentioned earlier, test anxiety often stems from lack of preparation, so the obvious solution is to prepare for the test. Effective studying may be the most important weapon you have for beating test anxiety, but you can and should employ several other mental tools to combat fear.

First, boost your confidence by reminding yourself of past success—tests or projects that you aced. If you're putting as much effort into preparing for this test as you did for those, there's no reason you should expect to fail here. Work hard to prepare; then trust your preparation.

Second, surround yourself with encouraging people. It can be helpful to find a study group, but be sure that the people you're around will encourage a positive attitude. If you spend time with others who are anxious or cynical, this will only contribute to your own anxiety. Look for others who are motivated to study hard from a desire to succeed, not from a fear of failure.

Third, reward yourself. A test is physically and mentally tiring, even without anxiety, and it can be helpful to have something to look forward to. Plan an activity following the test, regardless of the outcome, such as going to a movie or getting ice cream.

When you are taking the test, if you find yourself beginning to feel anxious, remind yourself that you know the material. Visualize successfully completing the test. Then take a few deep, relaxing breaths and return to it. Work through the questions carefully but with confidence, knowing that you are capable of succeeding.

Developing a healthy mental approach to test taking will also aid in other areas of life. Test anxiety affects more than just the actual test—it can be damaging to your mental health and even contribute to depression. It's important to beat test anxiety before it becomes a problem for more than testing.

## Study Strategy

Being prepared for the test is necessary to combat anxiety, but what does being prepared look like? You may study for hours on end and still not feel prepared. What you need is a strategy for test prep. The next few pages outline our recommended steps to help you plan out and conquer the challenge of preparation.

### Step 1: Scope Out the Test

Learn everything you can about the format (multiple choice, essay, etc.) and what will be on the test. Gather any study materials, course outlines, or sample exams that may be available. Not only will this help you to prepare, but knowing what to expect can help to alleviate test anxiety.

### Step 2: Map Out the Material

Look through the textbook or study guide and make note of how many chapters or sections it has. Then divide these over the time you have. For example, if a book has 15 chapters and you have five days to study, you need to cover three chapters each day. Even better, if you have the time, leave an extra day at the end for overall review after you have gone through the material in depth.

If time is limited, you may need to prioritize the material. Look through it and make note of which sections you think you already have a good grasp on, and which need review. While you are studying, skim quickly through the familiar sections and take more time on the challenging parts.

Write out your plan so you don't get lost as you go. Having a written plan also helps you feel more in control of the study, so anxiety is less likely to arise from feeling overwhelmed at the amount to cover.

## Step 3: Gather Your Tools

Decide what study method works best for you. Do you prefer to highlight in the book as you study and then go back over the highlighted portions? Or do you type out notes of the important information? Or is it helpful to make flashcards that you can carry with you? Assemble the pens, index cards, highlighters, post-it notes, and any other materials you may need so you won't be distracted by getting up to find things while you study.

If you're having a hard time retaining the information or organizing your notes, experiment with different methods. For example, try color-coding by subject with colored pens, highlighters, or post-it notes. If you learn better by hearing, try recording yourself reading your notes so you can listen while in the car, working out, or simply sitting at your desk. Ask a friend to quiz you from your flashcards, or try teaching someone the material to solidify it in your mind.

## Step 4: Create Your Environment

It's important to avoid distractions while you study. This includes both the obvious distractions like visitors and the subtle distractions like an uncomfortable chair (or a too-comfortable couch that makes you want to fall asleep). Set up the best study environment possible: good lighting and a comfortable work area. If background music helps you focus, you may want to turn it on, but otherwise keep the room quiet. If you are using a computer to take notes, be sure you don't have any other windows open, especially applications like social media, games, or anything else that could distract you. Silence your phone and turn off notifications. Be sure to keep water close by so you stay hydrated while you study (but avoid unhealthy drinks and snacks).

Also, take into account the best time of day to study. Are you freshest first thing in the morning? Try to set aside some time then to work through the material. Is your mind clearer in the afternoon or evening? Schedule your study session then. Another method is to study at the same time of day that you will take the test, so that your brain gets used to working on the material at that time and will be ready to focus at test time.

## Step 5: Study!

Once you have done all the study preparation, it's time to settle into the actual studying. Sit down, take a few moments to settle your mind so you can focus, and begin to follow your study plan. Don't give in to distractions or let yourself procrastinate. This is your time to prepare so you'll be ready to fearlessly approach the test. Make the most of the time and stay focused.

Of course, you don't want to burn out. If you study too long you may find that you're not retaining the information very well. Take regular study breaks. For example, taking five minutes out of every hour to walk briskly, breathing deeply and swinging your arms, can help your mind stay fresh.

As you get to the end of each chapter or section, it's a good idea to do a quick review. Remind yourself of what you learned and work on any difficult parts. When you feel that you've mastered the material, move on to the next part. At the end of your study session, briefly skim through your notes again.

But while review is helpful, cramming last minute is NOT. If at all possible, work ahead so that you won't need to fit all your study into the last day. Cramming overloads your brain with more information than it can process and retain, and your tired mind may struggle to recall even previously learned information when it is overwhelmed with last-minute study. Also, the urgent nature of cramming and the stress placed on your brain contribute to anxiety. You'll be more likely to go to the test feeling unprepared and having trouble thinking clearly.

So don't cram, and don't stay up late before the test, even just to review your notes at a leisurely pace. Your brain needs rest more than it needs to go over the information again. In fact, plan to finish your studies by noon or early afternoon the day before the test. Give your brain the rest of the day to relax or focus on other things, and get a good night's sleep. Then you will be fresh for the test and better able to recall what you've studied.

### Step 6: Take a Practice Test

Many courses offer sample tests, either online or in the study materials. This is an excellent resource to check whether you have mastered the material, as well as to prepare for the test format and environment.

Check the test format ahead of time: the number of questions, the type (multiple choice, free response, etc.), and the time limit. Then create a plan for working through them. For example, if you have 30 minutes to take a 60-question test, your limit is 30 seconds per question. Spend less time on the questions you know well so that you can take more time on the difficult ones.

If you have time to take several practice tests, take the first one open book, with no time limit. Work through the questions at your own pace and make sure you fully understand them. Gradually work up to taking a test under test conditions: sit at a desk with all study materials put away and set a timer. Pace yourself to make sure you finish the test with time to spare and go back to check your answers if you have time.

After each test, check your answers. On the questions you missed, be sure you understand why you missed them. Did you misread the question (tests can use tricky wording)? Did you forget the information? Or was it something you hadn't learned? Go back and study any shaky areas that the practice tests reveal.

Taking these tests not only helps with your grade, but also aids in combating test anxiety. If you're already used to the test conditions, you're less likely to worry about it, and working through tests until you're scoring well gives you a confidence boost. Go through the practice tests until you feel comfortable, and then you can go into the test knowing that you're ready for it.

## Test Tips

On test day, you should be confident, knowing that you've prepared well and are ready to answer the questions. But aside from preparation, there are several test day strategies you can employ to maximize your performance.

First, as stated before, get a good night's sleep the night before the test (and for several nights before that, if possible). Go into the test with a fresh, alert mind rather than staying up late to study.

Try not to change too much about your normal routine on the day of the test. It's important to eat a nutritious breakfast, but if you normally don't eat breakfast at all, consider eating just a protein bar. If you're a coffee drinker, go ahead and have your normal coffee. Just make sure you time it so that the caffeine doesn't wear off right in the middle of your test. Avoid sugary beverages, and drink enough water to stay hydrated but not so much that you need a restroom break 10 minutes into the test. If your test isn't first thing in the morning, consider going for a walk or doing a light workout before the test to get your blood flowing.

Allow yourself enough time to get ready, and leave for the test with plenty of time to spare so you won't have the anxiety of scrambling to arrive in time. Another reason to be early is to select a good seat. It's helpful to sit away from doors and windows, which can be distracting. Find a good seat, get out your supplies, and settle your mind before the test begins.

When the test begins, start by going over the instructions carefully, even if you already know what to expect. Make sure you avoid any careless mistakes by following the directions.

Then begin working through the questions, pacing yourself as you've practiced. If you're not sure on an answer, don't spend too much time on it, and don't let it shake your confidence. Either skip it and come back later, or eliminate as many wrong answers as possible and guess among the remaining ones. Don't dwell on these questions as you continue—put them out of your mind and focus on what lies ahead.

Be sure to read all of the answer choices, even if you're sure the first one is the right answer. Sometimes you'll find a better one if you keep reading. But don't second-guess yourself if you do immediately know the answer. Your gut instinct is usually right. Don't let test anxiety rob you of the information you know.

If you have time at the end of the test (and if the test format allows), go back and review your answers. Be cautious about changing any, since your first instinct tends to be correct, but make sure you didn't misread any of the questions or accidentally mark the wrong answer choice. Look over any you skipped and make an educated guess.

At the end, leave the test feeling confident. You've done your best, so don't waste time worrying about your performance or wishing you could change anything. Instead, celebrate the successful completion of this test. And finally, use this test to learn how to deal with anxiety even better next time.

**Review Video: Test Anxiety**
Visit mometrix.com/academy and enter code: 100340

## Important Qualification

Not all anxiety is created equal. If your test anxiety is causing major issues in your life beyond the classroom or testing center, or if you are experiencing troubling physical symptoms related to your anxiety, it may be a sign of a serious physiological or psychological condition. If this sounds like your situation, we strongly encourage you to seek professional help.

## Online Resources

Due to our efforts to try to keep this book to a manageable length, we've created a link that will give you access to all of your online resources:

mometrix.com/resources719/priisociology

# It's Your Moment, Let's Celebrate It!

**Share your story @mometrixtestpreparation**